OSPREY AIRCRAFT OF THE ACES • 5

Late Marque Spitfire Aces 1942 – 45

SERIES EDITOR: TONY HOLMES

OSPREY AIRCRAFT OF THE ACES • 5

Late Marque Spitfire Aces 1942 – 45

Dr Alfred Price

OSPREY
AEROSPACE

First published in Great Britain in Autumn 1995 by Osprey Publishing,
Elms Court, Chapel Way, Botley, Oxford, OX2 9LP

Reprinted Spring 1996
Reprinted Autumn 1998

ISBN 1 85532 575 6

Edited by Tony Holmes
Page design by TT Designs, Tony & Stuart Truscott

Cover Artwork by Iain Wyllie
Aircraft Profiles by Chris Davey, Keith Fretwell and Mark Rolfe
Figure Artwork by Mike Chappell
Scale Drawings by Mark Styling

Printed in Hong Kong

Front cover
**Sqn Ldr Otto Smik leads his flight of
Spitfire HF IXCs from No 312 'Czech'
Sqn into combat with a formation of
Bf 109Gs during a high level sweep
over north-western France in
September 1944. A Georgian by
birth, Smik fled to Britain following
the German occupation of his now
Slovakian home in 1938. Joining the
RAF soon after his arrival in England,
he served with distinction from 1942
with Nos 131, 122, 222 and 310 Sqns,
before being posted to No 312 Sqn in
September 1944 as a flight
commander, with eight kills to his
credit. Promoted to Squadron Leader
rank two months later, and given
charge of No 127 Sqn, Smik was
killed on 28 November 1944 during
fighter-bomber operations over
north-west Europe
(*Cover Painting by Iain Wyllie*)**

EDITOR'S NOTE
To make this new series as authoritative as possible, the editor would appreciate
hearing from any individual who may have relevant photographs, documenta-
tion or first-hand experiences relating to the elite pilots, and their aircraft, of the
various theatres of war. Any material used will be fully credited to its original
source. Please write to:
Tony Holmes, 1 Bradbourne Road, Sevenoaks, Kent, TN13 3PZ

CONTENTS

AUTHOR'S INTRODUCTION

Few will dispute the contention that the Spitfire was one of the most successful military aircraft ever built. In truth, no other aircraft design was ever developed so successfully, so continuously, so aggressively or so thoroughly as that of the Spitfire. As soon as the Spitfire Mk I entered service in the Royal Air Force the Supermarine company began a programme of incremental changes aimed at overcoming the new fighter's shortcomings. Also, for the longer term, the company launched a programme of more radical changes to improve its performance and fighting capability. The principal driving force behind this evolution was the work by Rolls-Royce engineers to increase the power developed by the Merlin engine. Each increase in power brought with it an increase in weight, however, usually accompanied by the need for a heavier propeller with more blades. And the problems did not end there. The hard-won lessons from combat imposed demands for improvements such as armour to protect the pilot, IFF equipment to identify the aircraft on radar, more effective (and heavier) radio equipment and a more powerful (and heavier) armament. To enable it to cope with these large increases in weight, the airframe had to be strengthened progressively (adding yet more weight) to enable it to maintain the pervious load factors.

Of course, the Spitfire would have amounted to nothing without the skills of the pilots who flew it in action. My purpose in writing this book is to show how the Spitfire evolved during the latter part of the war to allow it to take on the new threats from the enemy as they appeared, and how its capabilities were exploited by those who achieved ace status.

Several good friends contributed material and photographs to assist with the preparation of this book. In particular I am grateful to Ted Hooton, Norman Franks, Chaz Bowyer, Ray Sturtivant, Wojtek Matusiak, Zdenek Hurt, Geoff Thomas, Dr Jan P Koniarek, Jerry Scutts, Bruce Robertson, Neil Mackenzie and *Aeroplane Monthly*. Also, I should like to thank 'Hap' Kennedy for allowing me to quote the passage from his autobiography *Black Crosses off my Wingtip*. Finally, and most importantly, I convey my gratitude to Chris Shores for allowing me to use material from the latest edition of *Aces High* – for readers wishing to conduct further research on the RAF fighter aces, this book is strongly recommended.

Alfred Price
May 1995

A NEW AND MORE POTENT SPITFIRE

O n the afternoon of 30 July 1942 Flt Lt Donald Kingaby of No 64 Sqn scored his 16th aerial victory, and afterwards reported: 'I sighted approximately 12 Fw 190s 2000 ft below us at 12,000 ft just off Boulogne proceeding towards the French coast. We dived down on them and I attacked a Fw 190 from astern and below, giving a very short burst, about $^1/2$ sec, from 300 yds. I was forced to break away as I was crowded out by other Spits. I broke down and right and caught another Fw as he commenced to dive away. At 14,000 ft approx I gave a burst of cannon and M/G (machine guns), 400 yds range hitting E/A (enemy aircraft) along fuselage. Pieces fell off and E/A continued in straight dive nearly vertical. I followed E/A down to 5000 ft over Boulogne and saw him hit the deck outside the town of Boulogne and explode and burn up. Returned to base at 0 ft.'

Kingaby's report was little different from many others of that time, yet that action marked a significant turning point in the fortunes of Royal Air Force Fighter Command. This was the first occasion in which Spitfires had engaged the much-feared German Focke-Wulf Fw 190 fighter on equal terms. Kingaby and the other pilots in his squadron were taking the Spitfire Mk IX, the latest version of the famous fighter, in action for the first time. For the Luftwaffe, it was the beginning of the end of the air superiority its fighters had established over north-west Europe during the previous year.

The story begins ten months earlier in September 1941, when the Fw 190 first appeared over occupied France and the English Channel. The new German fighter was greatly superior to the Mk V Spitfire which equipped most of Fighter Command's day fighter units. The Fw 190 was more than 20 mph faster than the Spitfire V at all altitudes and it could out-climb, out-dive and out-roll the British fighter. During its offensive operations over occupied Europe, Fighter Command's losses rose alarmingly.

RAF fighter pilots were far from reticent about the qualities of their formidable new opponent. Their reports were relayed up the chain of command, gathering force as they did so, until they arrived on the desk of the Commander in Chief Fighter Command, Air Chief Marshal Sir Sholto Douglas. Adding his powerful voice to the clamour, Douglas wrote to the Ministry of Aircraft Production

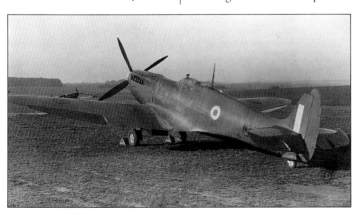

The unarmed Mk III Spitfire prototype N3297 was used as an engine test bed by Rolls-Royce, and is seen here after the installation of the Merlin 61 engine in the autumn of 1941. Once the teething troubles of the new powerplant had been overcome the improvement in performance led to the stop-gap Mk IX being rushed into production at the highest priority. This particular aircraft had initially been built by Vickers as part of an order for 200 Mk Is placed in 1937, and following it first flight in late 1939, it spent most of its life with Rolls-Royce demanding a fighter that could engage the Focke-Wulf from a position of equality or, preferably, of superiority. The Ministry, in its turn, relayed his demand to the aircraft manufacturers.

One answer would have been to design and build a completely new fighter to combat the Fw 190, but even on the most optimistic time scale it would have taken at least four years to bring it into service and Fighter Command couldn't afford to wait that long. Of the existing types, the Hawker Typhoon, then on the point of entering service, was as fast as the Fw 190 below 10,000 ft, but was suffering teething troubles, and above 20,000 ft was slower than the German fighter.

Fortunately for the RAF the solution to its most pressing problem was on the point of becoming a reality. Earlier in 1941, in response to a request to improve the high-altitude performance of the Merlin, Rolls-Royce engineers fitted a Merlin 45 (the engine that powered the Spitfire Mk V) with two supercharger blowers in series, one feeding into the other. Between the outlet of the first blower and the inlet of the second there was an extra cooling system – an intercooler – to reduce the temperature of the charge, and therefore increase its density.

The effect of the two-stage supercharger on the Merlin's high altitude performance was striking. At 30,000 ft the Merlin 45 with a normal single-stage supercharger developed about 720 horsepower. At the same altitude, the same basic engine with the two-stage supercharger developed about 1020 horsepower. The additional blower, the intercooler, and their respective casings, added only about 200 lbs to the weight of the Merlin 45 and increased its length by nine inches. The Merlin with two-stage supercharging was designated the Mark 60 and a revised version for installation in fighters was designated the Mk 61.

In the summer of 1941, shortly before the Fw 190 appeared on the scene, Rolls-Royce engineers fitted a Merlin 61 into Spitfire N3297, a Mk III employed as an engine test bed. The intercooler required its own radiator so the aircraft was modified with two oblong section radiator housings of similar external shape, one under each wing. The port housing contained the oil cooler radiator and half of the main coolant radiator, the starboard housing contained the intercooler radiator and the other half of the main coolant radiator. To absorb the Merlin 61's extra power, the aircraft was fitted with a four-bladed propeller.

The unarmed experimental Merlin 61 Spitfire made its first flight on 27 September 1941, just three weeks after the operational debut of the Fw 190. Initially there were problems with the intercooler, but by the end of the year the new engine was working satisfactorily. Early in 1942 the Spitfire went to the RAF test establishment at Boscombe Down for service trials, where it demonstrated a considerable improvement in performance compared with previous versions of the fighter: its maximum level speeds were recorded as 391 mph at 15,900 ft, 414 mph at 27,200 ft and 354 mph at 40,000 ft. Rate of climb was much superior to that of the Spitfire Mk V, and the new Spitfire's service ceiling was estimated at 41,800 ft.

THREE NEW VERSIONS

The promise of greatly improved performance from the new Merlin 61 engine spawned the development of three new versions of the Spitfire, the Mks VII, VIII and IX. The differences between them are set out in detail elsewhere in this volume, but essentially they were as follows.

The Mk VII was a dedicated high-altitude fighter with a pressurized cabin for the pilot. Based on the earlier Mk VI, it too was fitted with pointed wing tips which increased the span by 3 ft 4 ins and increased area by 6¹/₂ square feet. To provide sufficient fuel for a high speed climb to 40,000 ft perhaps followed by a lengthy tail chase, the internal fuel capacity of the Mk VII was raised to 124 gallons – 40 per cent more than previous Merlin-engined fighter versions of the Spitfire. The airframe of the Mk VII was also redesigned and strengthened to enable it cope with the extra weight and, to reduce drag, this version was fitted with a retractable tail wheel.

The second of the new variants, the Mk VIII, was essentially the same as the Mk VII except that it did not have the pressurised cabin, and it usually had the normal rounded wing tips. The task of redesigning the airframes of the Mks VII and VIII, and re-tooling the production lines to build them, took several months, however, and this delayed their entry into service.

Until the Mks VII and VIII became available in quantity, the RAF had a priority requirement for an interim version that would serve as a stop-gap counter to the Fw 190. This, the Mk IX, was essentially a Mk V with revised bearers to take the new engine and modified radiators under the wings. Other changes were restricted to the bare minimum necessary to allow the new fighter to perform effectively. The fact that the Mk IX's airframe was not fully stressed for operations, and that its all-up weight was greater than the Mk VII/VIII, was accepted on the grounds of operational expediency.

THE MK IX IN SERVICE

The first production Mk IXs were delivered in June 1942, and No 64 Sqn at Hornchurch duly became the premier unit to re-equip with the new variant. On 28 July it was declared operational, and after a couple of operations that saw no contact made with the enemy, Donald Kingaby gained the first victory in a Mk IX on the 30th (as described at the beginning of this section). Later that day the unit went into action again and claimed the destruction of a further three Fw 190s.

By the middle of August 1942 three more units had re-equipped with the Spitfire IX – Nos 401, 402 and No 611 Sqns. All four units were heavily committed in supporting the large-scale amphibious attack on Dieppe on the 19th.

The first to take-off soon after dawn were Nos 402 and 611 Sqns. Their task was to provide top cover for landing craft approaching the coast and fighters strafing designated ground targets along the shore. The Mk IXs had several inconclusive skirmishes with enemy fighters, without loss on either side.

AB196 started life as a Mk V, before becoming one of the earliest Mk IX conversions. It is seen here fitted with four 20 mm cannon, one of the few examples of this variant to be armed in this way *(via Oughton)*

During the mid-morning all four Mk IX units escorted B-17 Flying Fortresses attacking the fighter airfield at Abbeville. No 64 Sqn covered the bombers' withdrawal, while the other Spitfire IX units conducted a defensive sweep over the Dieppe beach head itself.

Nos 402 and 611 Sqns passed through the battle area without making contact with the enemy, but for No 401 Sqn it was a different story entirely. The Canadian unit found itself in action against Dornier Do 217s, escorted by Fw 190s, trying to attack shipping off the coast. The Spitfire IX pilots claimed hits on two bombers and one escort, but they did escape unscathed. Plt Off Don Morrison (who would reach ace status a few months later) headed after an Fw 190 he had seen about 1500 ft below him. In the Canadian official history *The RCAF Overseas: the First Four Years*, he described what happened next:

'I did a slipping barrel roll, losing height and levelled out about 150 yards behind and slightly to the starboard and above the enemy aircraft. I opened fire with a two-second burst closing to 25 yards. I saw strikes all along the starboard side of the fuselage and several pieces which seemed about a foot square flew off from around the cowling. Just as both the enemy aircraft and myself ran into cloud, he exploded with a terrific flash of flame and black smoke. I was quite unaware that

An impromptu low altitude fly-past by an anonymous squadron of Spitfire Mk IXs at a fighter station somewhere in the UK during 1943. This display may have marked the arrival of a newly re-equipped unit back at the frontline after converting onto type *(via Bruce Robertson)*

Early production F IXCs of No 611 'West Lancashire' Sqn in late 1942 cruise over South London in tight formation for the benefit of the Biggin Hill station photographer. This squadron was one of the first units to re-equip with the new Spitfire variant *(via Aeroplane)*

my own aircraft had been damaged (probably by flying debris) and was flying at about 1000 ft. Suddenly my engine started to cough and the aircraft shuddered violently. My engine cut out completely but I managed to reach 2000 ft. I took off my helmet, and undid my straps and opened the hood. I crouched on the seat and then shoved the stick forward. My parachute became caught somehow and I figured I was about 200-250 ft above the water when I got clear. The aircraft plunged into the water below me as my 'chute opened.'

After 15 minutes in the water Morrison was picked up by a naval patrol boat supporting the operation.

At midday all four Mk IX squadrons were again airborne, this time to cover the withdrawal of the Allied troops from the town. Nos 401, 402 and 611 Sqns were involved in skirmishes with German fighters, but No 64 found itself confronting another force of Do 217s attempting to bomb the ships. Sqn Ldr Duncan-Smith later reported:

'When leading squadron at 21,000 ft, flying south about five miles off Dieppe, I saw three Do 217s at about 5-6000 ft below also flying south. I led the squadron down and I attacked the left one of two who were rather close together. I gave a three-sec burst with cannon/machine gun from 250 yds, closed to point blank range, from port quarter closing to starboard and saw large pieces fly off the port engine, wing root and cockpit. When I broke away, the port engine had caught fire and flames were coming from the wing root and the cockpit. The aircraft dived almost vertically into cloud about 1000 ft below.'

Don Kingaby shot down another Do 217, his 19th victory. Duncan Smith shared another and Flt Lt Tommy Thomas damaged an Bf 109. In the course of the fast-moving action the squadron lost one Mk IX.

During the mid afternoon Nos 64, 402 and 611 Sqns were airborne again providing top cover for the withdrawing ships. Duncan Smith attacked another Do 217 and shot it down, but was hit by return fire from the rear gunner. Forced to bail out, he was rescued from the sea by a naval vessel. The aircraft he abandoned was BR581, the first Mk IX delivered to the unit – its operational life had lasted just 23 days.

In the course of the day's intensive air fighting the four Spitfire Mk IX units put up 14 squadron-sized missions with a total of about 150 sorties, and they claimed six enemy aircraft destroyed and two probably destroyed for the loss of seven of their number. The break-down of missions, claims and losses was as follows:

Spitfire F IXCs of No 340 'Ile de France' Sqn are captured on film moments before take-off from Biggin Hill – the Free French unit had only recently swapped its Mk Vs for IXBs when this photograph was taken in October 1942. Following the completion of its tour at Biggin in March 1943, No 340 Sqn was despatched to Turnhouse and Drem for a period of rest, where it was again issued with Mk VBs (via Aeroplane)

Out on patrol over the Channel in 1944, four Spitfire Mk IXs of No 313 'Czech' Sqn each boast a 90-gallon long-range slipper tank under the fuselage. Like No 340 Sqn, this unit had flown Spitfire Mk VB/Cs and Mk VIs from late 1941 to early 1944 from various airfields in the UK, prior to receiving Mk IXs at Ibsley in February 1944 (Klimet)

No 64 Sqn flew three missions, claimed four Do 217s destroyed; lost three aircraft.

No 401 Sqn flew three missions, claimed one Fw 190 destroyed and two probably destroyed, three Do 217s and four Fw 190s damaged; lost three aircraft and one returned damaged.

No 402 Sqn flew four missions, claimed three Fw 190 damaged; no losses

No 611 Sqn flew four missions, claimed one Fw 190 destroyed and two damaged; lost one aircraft.

──── COMBAT IN THE STRATOSPHERE ────

Even as the air battles were being fought out over Dieppe, the Luftwaffe was making final preparations to open a new phase in its attack on targets in England. A few days later the *Höhenkampfkommando* (High Altitude Bomber Detachment), with two Junkers Ju 86R bombers, arrived at Beauvais in northern France in readiness to commence operations.

The Ju 86R was powered by two turbo-supercharged diesel engines with nitrous oxide injection to provide increased power at ultra-high altitudes. The bomber was not fast, with a maximum speed of just over 200 mph, but with its long, pointed, wing spanning 105 ft it could reach altitudes around 45,000 ft. That, it was thought, would enable it to attack targets in Britain with impunity by day. The aircraft's bomb load consisted of a solitary 550-lb bomb, but the main consideration for the Luftwaffe was to derive as much propaganda value as possible from a series of daylight attacks against which the British air defences would be seen to be helpless. The Ju 86Rs delivered their first attack on 24 August when one aircraft bombed Camberley and the other Southampton. Fighter Command scrambled 15 Spitfire Mk Vs, but they all failed to intercept the high flying bombers.

On the following day one of the bombers returned and flew a meandering course that took it over Southampton and then to the north of London, setting off air raid sirens and causing people to take shelter over a wide swathe of south-east England. The single bomb was dropped on Stansted, then it flew past the east side of London and left

'BF273', the Mk IX flown by Flg Off Emanuel Galitzine of the High Altitude Flight at Northolt during the combat with a Ju 86R of the *Höhenkampfkommando* at 43,500 ft over Southampton on 12 September 1942 – this intercept was the highest recorded air combat of World War 2. At the time of the action this aircraft had been specially modified for operations at extreme altitudes with the machine guns, armour and other unnecessary items of equipment removed, and the airframe painted PRU blue overall. 'BF273' was applied in error by the groundcrew of this aircraft, as this serial was one of a block actually allocated to Blenheims – the aircraft was later given its correct serial, BS273 *(via Hooton)*

the coast at Shoreham. Nine Spitfires Vs were scrambled, but again they failed to get anywhere near the intruder.

In the following two-and-a half weeks the Ju 86Rs flew nine sorties over England, still without encountering effective fighter interference. The high-flying bombers' spell of invulnerability was fast drawing to a close, however. Having assessed the nature of the threat Fighter Command ordered the formation of a new unit, the Special Service Flight at Northolt, to deal with the menace.

The ideal counter to the Ju 86R would have been the Spitfire VII, but this version was not yet ready for operations. As an interim measure the Flight received two Mk IXs specially lightened for high altitude operations. All armour and unnecessary equipment was removed. So were the four machine guns, leaving an armament of just two 20 mm Hispano cannon.

On 12 September one of the Ju 86Rs headed over the English Channel for its next attack, but this time the defenders were ready. Flg Off Emanuel Galitzine was scrambled to intercept, and after a rapid climb to 40,000 ft he caught sight of the bomber over the Solent, in a slightly higher position off his starboard wing. At about the same time the German crew saw him, and the pilot jettisoned the bomb and selected full power in an attempt to out climb the fighter.

The lightened Spitfire was able to climb faster, however, and its pilot moved into an attacking position above and behind the Ju 86R:

'I positioned myself for an attack and dived to about 200 yards astern of him, where I opened up with a three-second burst. At the end of the burst my port cannon jammed and the Spitfire slewed round to starboard; then, as I passed through the bomber's slipstream, my canopy misted over. The canopy took about a minute to clear completely, during which time I climbed back into position for the next attack. When I next saw the Junkers it was heading southwards, trying to escape out to sea. I knew I had to get right in close behind him if I was to stand any chance of scoring hits, because it would be difficult to hold the Spitfire straight when the starboard cannon fired and she went into a yaw. Again I dived to attack but when I was about a hundred yards away the bomber went into a surprisingly tight turn to starboard. I opened fire but the Spitfire went into a yaw and fell out of the sky; I broke off the attack, turned outside him and climbed back to 44,000 ft.'

By clever manoeuvring the bomber crew avoided the next two attacks, then Galitzine lost sight of his opponent in a patch of mist. Now starting to run short of fuel, he turned away and landed at Tangmere.

The Ju 86R landed at Caen with holes where a 20 mm armour-piercing round had passed through the port wing. The German crew's report of the interception made it clear that the Spitfire had been able to outclimb the Ju 86R. The latter was no longer immune from fighter attack and, less than three weeks after they started, the operations by the *Höhenkampfkommando* were brought to a abrupt end.

The action between Galitzine's Spitfire and the Ju 86R on 12 September 1942 would be the highest air-to-air combat to be fought during World War 2.

Flg Off Emanuel Galitzine piloted the modified Mk IX during the epic high altitude combat of 12 September 1942 *(Galitzine)*

Wg Cdr Harold Bird-Wilson, leader of No 122 Wg based at Funtington in January 1944. At the end of the war his victory score stood at three enemy aircraft destroyed and six shared destroyed, three damaged and one destroyed on the ground *(Bird-Wilson via Norman Franks)*

New Zealander Sqn Ldr John Mackenzie was given command of No 64 Sqn in April 1944. An ex-Battle of Britain pilot, his final score stood at six enemy aircraft destroyed, four probably destroyed and two damaged – all were achieved while flying early mark Spitfires, however *(Bird-Wilson via Norman Franks)*

THE SPITFIRE MK IXB, ALIAS LF IX

During the mid-war period new sub-variants of the Spitfire sometimes reached the squadrons before an official designation had been allocated, with the result that the fighter pilots coined their own unofficial designation. An example of this occurred in the spring of 1943 when the Spitfire Mk IX entered service powered by the new Merlin 66 engine. Compared with the Merlin 61 this engine had the two supercharger gears arranged to cut-in at slightly lower altitudes, and thus provide the best possible performance at each altitude compared with the Fw 190.

When the new Mk IXs were delivered to units, pilots needed a means of differentiating it from the earlier aircraft powered by the Merlin 61 or 63, so the new sub-variant was called the 'Mark IXB', and earlier Spitfire Mk IXs with Merlin 61 or 63 engines became known as 'Mk IXAs' – some sources have suggested that the 'A' and 'B' designations referred to the armament fitted to the aircraft, but this was not the case.

When Wg Cdr Alan Deere took command of the Biggin Hill Wing in the spring of 1943 it had just re-equipped with Mk IXs fitted with Merlin 66s. In his autobiographical classic *Nine Lives* he described the new sub-variant of the Spitfire in enthusiastic terms:

'I was now all set to renew my acquaintance with the formidable Focke Wulf, but this time I was better equipped. The Biggin Hill squadrons were using the *Spitfire IXB (Merlin 66)* (author's italics), a mark of Spitfire markedly superior in performance to the Fw 190 below 27,000 ft.

'Unlike the Spitfire IXA, with which all other Spitfire IX Wings in the Group were equipped, the IXB's supercharger came in at a lower altitude and the aircraft attained its best performance at 22,000 ft, or at roughly the same altitude as the Fw 190. At this height it was approximately 30 mph faster, was better in the climb and vastly more manoeuvrable.'

Later in the year the Ministry of Aircraft Production introduced three new official designations for sub-variants of the Mk IX in an attempt to resolve the position. They were as follows:

F IXC (unofficially referred to as the 'Mk IXA') – aircraft fitted with Merlin 61, 63 or 63A engines, with the C type wing and armament.

LF IXC (unofficially referred to as the 'Mk IXB') – aircraft fitted with the Merlin 66 engine and with C type wing and armament; although the LF designation implied that this version was optimized for low altitude operations, in fact its high altitude performance was only slightly reduced and it developed its maximum speed at 22,000 ft (compared with 28,000 ft for the F Mk IX).

HF IXC – version fitted with the Merlin 70 engine, with the C type wing and armament provision. This version was optimised for operations at extreme altitude.

The official edict reached the frontline long after the designations 'Mk IXA' and 'Mk IXB' had become established at the squadrons. As a result, pilots' logbooks and unit record books continued to use the unofficial designations wherever it was thought appropriate.

Mк IXs
In the Mediterranean Theatre

The entry into service of the Spitfire Mk IX enabled RAF Fighter Command to regain the air superiority it had lost over north west Europe to the Fw 190. In the Mediterranean theatre it was the same story, though not until the Mk IX arrived there early in 1943. The first unit to receive it, No 81 Sqn based at Constantine in Algeria, went into action with its new aircraft on 31 January, and soon afterwards a second unit, No 72 Sqn based at Souk el Kemis in Tunisia, also received Mk IXs.

At the same time the Desert Air Force to the east of Tunisia received an important addition to its ranks with the arrival of the Polish Fighting Team. Equipped with Mk IXs, this elite 15-pilot volunteer unit was led in the air by Sqn Ldr Stanislaw Skalski, and included such famous names as Karol Pniak, Waclaw Krol, Eugeniusz Horbaczewski and Kazimierz Sporney. For administrative purposes the 'Team' was attached to No 145 Sqn based at Ben Gardane, and its aircraft carried that unit's ZX code letters, though with an individual number instead of a letter. Between the arrival of the unit and the surrender of the last of the Axis forces in North Africa on 13 May, Horbaczewski added five victories to his score and Skalski and Sporny each added three each victories to theirs'.

During the campaign in Tunisia two Fighter Groups belonging to the US 12th Air Force operated with Spitfire Mk Vs; the 31st (comprising the 307th, 308th and 309th Fighter Squadrons); and the 52nd

Norwegian Maj Helge Mehre led No 132 Wg, based at Bognor, from late 1943 until the end of the war. By May 1945 his victory score stood at six enemy aircraft destroyed and ten damaged – four Fw 190s were destroyed and four damaged by Mehre whilst flying the Mk IX *(via Norman Franks)*

Spitfire Mk IX ZX-6 flown by Sqn Ldr Stanislaw Skalski, commander of the Polish Fighting Team (PFT) – or 'Skalski's Circus' as they were colloquially known – attached to No 145 Sqn and operating in Tunisia in the spring of 1943. With the Afrika Korps in full retreat by this stage, and the remnants of the Luftwaffe in-threatre attempting to stem the overwhelming Allied forces, the PFT found no shortage of targets whilst in North Africa. First seeing combat on 28 March, the 15 pilots of C Flight went on to down 25 German and Italian aircraft for the loss of one pilot shot down and captured up to end of the campaign on 13 May *(IWM)*

This Spitfire Mk IX of No 4 Sqn, South Africa Air Force, was photographed at Gerbini, Sicily, in September 1943. Seasoned campaigners in North Africa, this unit had fought from 1941 onwards across Egypt, Libya and Tunisia in Tomahawks and Kittyhawks, prior to receiving the vastly superior Spitfire Mk IX in July 1943 *(Aeroplane)*

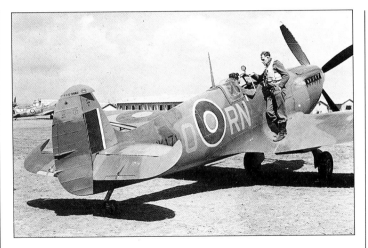

Spitfire LF IX of No 72 Sqn at Lago, Italy, in late 1944

(comprising the 2nd, 4th and 5th Fighter Squadrons). Towards the end of April 1943 the RAF turned over some of its precious Mk IXs to these US Groups, and the latter then flew them in action.

During the months that followed the Axis capitulation in Tunisia, the number of Mk IX-equipped RAF units in the theatre built up rapidly. Also, the US 31st and 52nd Fighter Groups re-equipped fully with this variant, and operated it until the spring of 1944.

THE SPITFIRE MK VII IN SERVICE

Due to the low rate of production of the Mk VII, No 124 Sqn at North Weald took until May 1943 to become fully operational with the variant. The Mk VII scored its first success on the 15th of that month when Flg Off Willis carried out a successful interception of an Fw 190 at 38,000 ft near Plymouth and shot it down.

In August 1943 three Mk VIIs were allocated to the Station Flight at Skeabrae in the Orkney Islands to engage German high altitude reconnaissance aircraft attempting to photograph the fleet anchorage at Scapa Flow. Fighter squadrons based in southern England were rotated through the airfield for rest periods lasting about three months, and the Mk VIIs were flown by pilots from the unit detached to Skeabrae, but the occasions for action were few and far between.

Stanislaw Skalski, seen here late in the war when he held the rank of Wing Commander, opened his score flying a PZL 11c fighter over Poland in 1939, when he was credited with the destruction of six enemy aircraft. At the end of the war he was the top-scoring Polish pilot with 21 (some sources say 24) enemy aircraft destroyed, one probably destroyed and five damaged (Koniarek Archives)

Flt Lt Eugeniusz Horbaczewski (above right) flew with the Polish Fighting Team in Tunisia in the spring of 1943. He was later promoted to Squadron Leader and commanded No 315 Sqn equipped with Mustangs, but was shot down and killed on 16 August 1944 during a one-sided combat with 60 Fw 190s over France – he downed three before being mortally wounded. At the time of his death his score stood at 16 enemy aircraft destroyed and one shared destroyed, one probably destroyed and one damaged (Koniarek Archives)

Spitfire Mk IX of the 309th FS, 31stFG in Tunisia in early May 1943 (via Ethell)

A line up of Spitfire Mk IXs of the 309th FS, 31st FG, which were part of the US 12th Air Force at Castel Volturno, near Casino in Italy, in March 1944 – in the background are P-51Bs which had just arrived to replace them. Note that in this unit it was standard practice to duplicate each aircraft's identification letter on the fuselage (*via Ethell*)

Spitfire Mk IX of No 242 Sqn taxying in at Calenzana, in Corsica, after returning from a sortie over the invasion area in the south of France in August 1944 (*via Aeroplane*)

Lt Col R Rogers (standing), commander of No 40 Sqn South African Air Force, with his distinctively marked Spitfire Mk IX PT672 at an airfield in Italy (*via Bruce Robertson*)

Flg Off Otto Smik of No 222 Sqn with his Mk IX in 1943. He was killed in action in November 1944 when his score stood at eight enemy aircraft destroyed and two shared destroyed, two probably destroyed and three damaged, plus three V1s destroyed during the mid-summer of 1944 (*van der Meer*)

17

In September 1943 a second unit was equipped with the Mk VII, No 616 Sqn at Exeter, and in March 1944 a third unit received the variant, No 131 Sqn at Colerne. A total of 140 Mk VIIs were built at the Supermarine factories in the Southampton area, the last being delivered in May 1944.

During the preparations for the Normandy invasion Nos 131 and 616 Sqns formed part of the Culmhead Wing commanded by Battle of Britain ace Wg Cdr Peter Brothers. As well as protecting the invasion ports from high flying German reconnaissance aircraft, which appeared only rarely, the Mk VIIs were to provide top cover during the invasion.

In this context 'top cover' proved to be a relative term, however. If there was a need for high cover, at whatever level, the Spitfire Mk VIIs provided it, though usually its aircraft patrolled at altitudes around 20,000 ft. With the absence of high altitude 'trade', the Mk VIIs came to be operated like ordinary Spitfires. Indeed, in the days following the invasion the Mk VIIs strafed road and rail targets and, on occasions, airfields. Since there was no requirement for Mk VIIs to operate at high altitude, two

This Spitfire Mk VII was allocated to the Station Flight at Skeabrae, in the Orkney Islands, for the purpose of engaging high-altitude reconnaissance aircraft attempting to photograph the fleet anchorage at Scapa Flow. Although the aircraft bears the markings of No 312 Sqn, after that unit left the airfield it was flown by pilots from other units based in southern England which rotated through the airfield for rest periods lasting about three months. In February 1944 Flt Lt Ian Blair of No 602 Sqn was flyimg this aircraft when he shot down a Bf 109 reconnaissance fighter. The photograph shows well the extended span wing, pointed tips and reduced span ailerons of this variant *(Blair)*

weeks after D-Day it was decided to replace the pointed tips with standard rounded ones, which gave better manoeuvrability at low-level. The pointed tips saw little further use.

Peter Brothers led a 'Rodeo' sweep by No 131 Sqn over northern France on 7 August 1944. Flying as his wingman was Sqn Ldr 'Sammy' Sampson, an experienced pilot serving as a Staff Officer at No 10 Grp HQ between tours. They encountered six Fw 190s and set off in pursuit at low-level. Brothers describes the one-sided action that followed:

Spitfire Mk VII of No 131 Sqn, pictured in the spring of 1944 when the unit was at Culmhead as part of Peter Brothers' wing *(Nicholson)*

'It was a long haul to catch up with them, and during the pursuit I realised that the pilot of the aircraft I had singled out really hadn't got a clue. All he did to shake me off was make gentle turns to the left and right, which slowed him down a fair bit and thus allowed me to catch him up even quicker . . .

After a hectic chase at about 250 ft off the deck Sammy and I finally came within firing distance of our respective targets and gave them quick bursts of cannon, which clobbered them both. One of my rounds went straight into the cockpit of the Fw 190, no doubt killing its occupant instantly. It really was quite horrific as I always preferred to knock off part of the wing or set the engine ablaze, which gave the pilot a sporting chance of bailing out or crash landing. This action left an unpleasant taste in my mouth.

'We often met enemy aircraft on our long-range missions, occasionally bouncing them at their home airfields. On one particularly successful attack in August 1944 we hit the airfields at Le Valle and Le Mans, catching the former base by total surprise and hitting many Fw 190s on the ground. By the time we reached the latter airfield word had been radioed to the incumbents from Le Valle of our impending visit, and most of the fighters on the base were in the process of taking off when we roared overhead at low-level. I claimed a Fw 190 taking off, which was really quite unfair as the chap had barely got his wheels in the gear wells when I shot him down. Indeed, we inflicted so much damage on that sortie that the Wing got a letter of congratulations from the C-in-C.

'We also flew daylight bomber escort missions in our long-range Spits, with three-and-a-half-hour sortie becoming quite commonplace. Quite often, the hardest thing we faced on these endurance sorties was the dinghy we sat on, which become extremely uncomfortable after a while! On one raid, in which we had 250 Lancasters under our protection, I remember that my number two and I had taken the very tail of the formation. The remainder of my two squadrons were split into pairs on either side of the bomber stream from the mid way point back, whilst Wg Cdr "Birdy" Bird-Wilson had his Harrowbeer Wing spread over the front half of the formation. Just to emphasise how physically large our task was, whilst I was talking to "Birdy" on the R/T he was passing over the Channel Islands and I was just leaving the suburbs of Bordeaux with the tail end of the column!

Shortly after this No 616 Sqn re-equipped with Meteor jet fighters, then No 124 Sqn re-equipped with Mk IXs. That left No 131 Sqn as the sole unit equipped with the Mk VII, and it continued with the same pattern of operations as before.

With an internal fuel capacity of 129 gallons, nearly half as much

Wg Cdr Peter Brothers, commander of the Culmhead Wing in the summer of 1944. An ex-Battle of Britain Hurricane pilot, Brothers had been credited with 16 enemy aircraft destroyed, one probably destroyed and three damaged by the end of the war

A Mk VII Spitfire of No 131 Sqn seen in August 1944. This aircraft has shed its high-altitude overall grey scheme in favour of normal day fighter camouflage, although it still carries invasion stripes on the lower surfaces. It has also had the distinctive Mk VII pointed wing tips removed and normal rounded ones fitted in their place. Operating Mk VIIs alongside No 131 Sqn from Culmhead was No 616 Sqn, with the final unit within the wing being the Mk XII-equipped No 41 Sqn (via Bruce Robertson)

Flt Lt James 'Eddie' Edwards hailed from Saskatchewan, Canada, and by the time this shot was taken in 1944, he had already seen two years of action in Kittyhawks in North Africa. He flew Spitfire Mk VIIIs with No 417 'City of Windsor' Sqn, RCAF, in Italy in late 1943, before being sent to No 92 Sqn as a flight commander. Edwards' final score was 15 aircraft destroyed and 3 shared, 8 and 1 shared probably destroyed and 13 damaged, 9 destroyed on the ground and 5 damaged on the ground

again as the Mk IXs then in service, the Mk VII was sometimes used as a bomber escort. On 11 August No 131 Sqn flew its longest range operation of this type when it escorted Lancasters delivering a daylight attack on submarine pens at La Pallice. The 690-mile round trip took 3 hours 50 minutes. That was close to the Mk VII's maximum radius of action, which meant that there was little spare fuel to engage in combat if enemy fighters attacked the bombers. The high-level escorts flew throttled back keeping above their charges, hoping that by their presence they would deter enemy fighters from interfering. Fortunately for the Mk VII pilots, the stratagem succeeded on this occasion.

The Mk VII passed out of service in January 1945 without having had the chance to prove its capabilities as a high-altitude interceptor.

THE SPITFIRE MK VIII IN MEDITERRANEAN SERVICE

The entry into service of the Mk IX reduced the urgency to get the dedicated Mk VIII/Merlin 61 version into mass-production. The first Mk VIII came off the Supermarine production line in November 1942, but it was June 1943 before production exceeded 50 per month. The Mk VIII had the same internal fuel capacity as the Mk VII – 124 gallons – and it was decided that the entire production be sent to units in the Mediterranean and Far Eastern theatres. The need to ship the aircraft to these distant theatres further delayed its service introduction, and the first unit to receive it, No 145 Sqn in Malta, only became operational only in June 1943.

In addition to the deliveries of Mk VIIIs to RAF units in Italy, the US Army Air Forces received a total of 55 examples which were operated together with Mk Vs by the 308th FS of the 31st FG – the remaining squadrons in the Group retained their Mk IXs and Mk Vs.

In the spring of 1944 the role of Allied Spitfire units in the Mediterranean theatre equipped with Mk VIIIs and IXs shifted gradually from that of air superiority to fighter-bomber.

The Mk VIII Spitfire had provision for the fitting of either pointed wing tips for high altitude operations or normal wing tips. This No 417 Sqn machine, based at Lentini in Italy in the summer of 1943, operated with pointed tips (Public Archives of Canada)

Groundcrew refuel a No 92 Sqn Mk VIII with pointed tips at Grottaglie, near Taranto, in southern Italy in September 1943. Note the triangular squadron emblem in front of the cockpit, which was painted on both sides of the fuselage (via Aeroplane)

Spitfire Mk VIII of No 601 Sqn, pictured at an airfield in Italy in the spring of 1944. The unit's 'Flying Sword' emblem was painted on the white disc at the top of the fin (via Bruce Robertson)

A Spitfire Mk VIII of No 417 Sqn seen at a damp Venafro, in Italy, in April 1944. This aircraft had earlier served with the 308th FS of the USAAF's 31st FG, and when the former re-equipped with P-51Bs the Spitfire was returned to the RAF (Public Archives of Canada)

This Spitfire Mk VIII of No 253 Sqn has clipped wings, a fit rarely observed on the Mk VIII despite it being a common mod on other marks of the Supermarine fighter. Here, it is seen undergoing basic field servicing at Prkos, Yugoslavia, in early 1945 (via Bruce Robertson)

Above and right Mk VIIIs of No 43 Sqn are seen at a forward landing ground in southern France – probably Ramatuelle, near St Tropez – in August 1944. The three aircraft being prepared for a mission are each armed with a 500-lb bomb *(via Bruce Robertson and via Aeroplane)*

These Mk VIIIs of the 308th FS, 31st FG, US 12th Air Force, are about to take-off from Castel Volturno, Italy, in early 1944 *(via Ethell)*

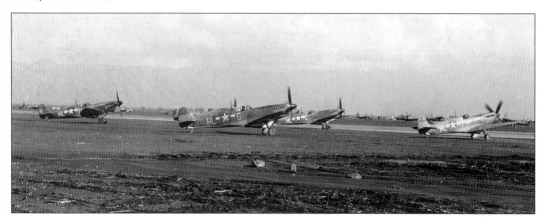

THE SPITFIRE MK VIII IN SOUTH-EAST ASIAN SERVICE

In the Far East the first Mk VIIIs arrived towards the end of 1943, with the first two units to receive this variant being Nos 81 and 152 Sqns based at Alipore and Baigachi in eastern India. Early in 1944 two other units became operational with the variant, No 67 Sqn at Chittagong and No 155 Sqn at Alipore. At that time there were three Mk V squadrons based close to the frontline, Nos 136 and 607 Sqns at Ramu and No 615 Sqn at Chittagong.

Initially there was little air activity over the theatre. By that stage of the war the Japanese Army Air Force was badly over-stretched, and its few units in Burma had to conserve their strength. The main source of excitement come from the occasional Mitsubishi Ki 46 'Dinah' recon-

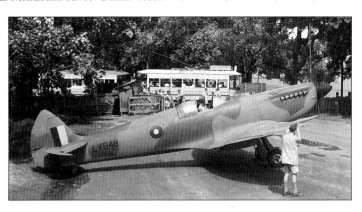

Newly re-assembled and painted, this Mk VIII Spitfire seen at an RAF maintenance unit near Calcutta, was being ground run prior to taking off for its first air test after uncrating in the spring of 1944. This aircraft later saw service with No 67 Sqn as the unit pushed eastward in support of Gen Slim's 14th Army, who were harassing the retreating Japanese army as it stubbornly pulled out of Burma *(via Bruce Robertson)*

naissance aircraft making a high-speed dash through Allied territory at high altitude to photograph troop positions and other targets. Previously the Ki 46s had operated with near-impunity, but following the arrival of the Spitfire Mk VIIIs the Japanese reconnaissance units had suffered mounting losses.

The period of relative calm ended on 6 February when Japanese troops launched a major offensive in the Arakan area. The attackers used the well-tried tactic of infiltrating forces through the jungle to get behind the Allied positions, thus severing their supply routes and forcing the troops to pull back. But this time Gen William Slim, commander of the British 14th Army, used a new counter-tactic. Relying on the new Spitfires to establish air superiority over the battle area, he ordered the cut off troops at Sinzweya to stand firm. The 5000 men surrounded there were to be supplied from the air by Dakota and C-46 Commando transports until they could be relieved.

The three Spitfire Mk VIII units, each commanded by a fighter ace, moved to the forward airfield at Ramu, close to the Indian-Burmese

Another Mk VIII Spitfire of No 67 Sqn touches down at Comilla, in India, in July 1944. This large airfield served as home for the squadron between July and November 1944, with the unit also operating small flight-strength (four aircraft) detachments to Chittagong and Cox's Bazaar throughout their stay at Comilla *(via Aeroplane)*

Tackling the mud, Spitfire Mk VIII pilots from No 607 'County of Durham' Sqn return from a sortie, at Kalaywa, in Burma, in the late spring of 1945. The photograph shows well the South-East Asia Command white stripes painted on the wings and tail surfaces. These aircraft were camouflaged in the familiar dark green and dark earth scheme worn in this theatre. Although the Mk VIIIs were heavily involved in wresting aerial supremacy from the Japanese Army Air Force over the Imphal fortress in mid-1944, by early 1945 no airborne enemy aircraft had been sighted for months. Therefore the unit turned to the fighter-bomber role, principally in support of the push into Rangoon *(via Bruce Robertson)*

Flg Off Wilfred Goold of No 607 Sqn pictured in the cockpit of his Spitfire Mk VIII in May 1944. Having learnt to fly with the RAAF in his native Australia in 1940/41, Goold was posted to Britain where he joined No 607 Sqn. He was then sent to India with the unit, and took part in the retreat from Burma, scoring his first kill along the way – all of his claims were against 'Oscars'. By the time No 607 went back on the offensive in 1944 it had lost it Hurricane IICs in favour of Spitfire VCs and then VIIIs. Goold claimed four aircraft destroyed, one probably destroyed and five damaged whilst flying Spits *(via Norman Franks)*

Spitfire Mk VIIIs of No 152 Sqn, photographed in July 1945 at Thedaw, in Burma *(via Norman Franks)*

border, to support the airlift: No 67 Sqn (Sqn Ldr Thomas Parker), No 81 Sqn (Sqn Ldr William Whitamore) and No 152 Sqn (Sqn Ldr Mervin Ingram). The arrival of these units changed the air situation completely. The Spitfire Mk V had been about equal in performance to the best Japanese fighter in the theatre, the Nakajima Ki 44 'Tojo'. However, the Spitfire Mk VIII had a speed advantage of 40 mph over the Ki 44, and 90 mph over the more numerous Nakajima Ki 43-II 'Oscar'. The Spitfires inflicted such heavy losses on the JAAF that after a few days the latter ceased operations over the battle area, and the airlift proceeded unhindered.

As the battle front stabilised, the Japanese infiltration tactics rebounded on them. Their troops had advanced on foot over jungle trails, and when they had eaten the food they carried they were expected to sustain themselves on whatever they could capture from the enemy. That strategy failed when the defenders, supplied from the air, held on to their positions. The Japanese lacked any effective means of transporting supplies to their troops in the jungle some distance behind the frontline, and after three weeks the starving infiltrators were

Spitfire Mk VIIIs of No 136 Sqn, based in the Cocos Islands in the summer of 1945. One of the first fighter units despatched to Burma in the dark days of early 1942, No 136 Sqn was virtually wiped out during the retreat back into India, its weary Hurricane IIAs and Bs proving no match for the Japanese Army Ki 27 'Nate' and Ki 43 'Oscar' fighters. No 136 Sqn eventually received Spitfire VCs in October 1943, and then Mk VIIIs three months later. By VJ Day, the unit had scored more kills than any other RAF squadron in-theatre *(via Bruce Robertson)*

MV483, one of the final production Mk VIIIs, served with No 155 Sqn in Burma in 1945

forced to withdraw. The seige was finally lifted on 23 February. The action at Sinzweya formed the pattern for Slim's counter to the main Japanese offensive in Burma, mounted the following month, when he used a much larger airlift to supply the 55,000 troops cut off at Kohima and Imphal. Again the Spitfire Mk VIIIs maintained air supremacy, and throughout the 80-day airlift operation only three Allied transport aircraft were lost to enemy action. By the end of the seige Nos 136, 607 and 615 Sqns had also re-equipped with the Spitfire Mk VIII, strengthening the RAF's hold on air superiority Burma. Never again would the Japanese Army Air Force be able to pose a serious challenge to that position.

THE SPITFIRE MK VIII IN SERVICE IN AUSTRALIA AND THE SOUTH PACIFIC

The Royal Australian Air Force (RAAF) received a total of 410 Mk VIIIs, with the first batch arriving at the port of Melbourne in October

1943. Five squadrons in the south Pacific area equipped with this type, Nos 54, 79, 452, 453, 548 and 549.

In the summer of 1945 No 80 Wing RAAF, commanded by leading Australian fighter ace Grp Capt Clive Caldwell, and comprising Nos 79, 452 and 453 Sqns, transferred to bases in New Guinea. Despite many of these units boasting squadron and flight commanders of ace status, by this time Japanese air activity over the south-west Pacific area had virtually ended. The Wing had little opportunity for air-to-air combat and was used mainly in the ground-strafing role.

THE MK XVI IN SERVICE

The Mk XVI was a Mk IX airframe fitted with the Merlin 266 engine,

Newly delivered clipped-winged Spitfire Mk XVIEs of No 74 Sqn at Schijndel, in Holland, in March 1945 await the painting of the unit's 4D identification letters on their umarked fuselages. The nearest aircraft is TB859, and stacked in the foreground are jettisonable 30-gallon slipper tanks ready for use. The Spitfires carry the standard load of two 250-lb bombs under the wings and a single 500-lb device under the fuselage *(Murland)*

More Mk XVIEs of No 74 Sqn are prepared for a sortie as they sit at their PSP (pierced steel planking) dispersal point at Schijndel in the spring of 1945 *(Murland)*

The Spitfire Mk XVIEs of No 74 Sqn were powered by Packard-built Merlin 266s, and were amongst the first with 'rear-view' fuselages to reach frontline RAF units. The licence-built engines were constructed to US measurements, and as a result required different servicing tools from those used by their Rolls-Royce counterparts. Here, groundcrewmen are tweaking the engine on a bombed-up aircraft prior to declaring the machine serviceable for its next mission *(Murland)*

Bombs gone, a fighting pair of Spitfire Mk XVIEs from the 'Tiger' Squadron return to B105/Droppe, in western Germany, in April 1945 following one of the unit's last missions of the war *(Murland)*

This Mk XVI of No 322 Sqn, photographed at an airfield in Holland early in 1945, has clipped wings but retains the familiar solid Mk IX-type fuselage *(via Aeroplane)*

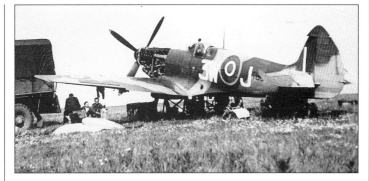

Spitfire Mk XVIEs of No 443 'Hornet' Sqn pictured over their base at Schneverdingen, in Germany, in April 1945 – the code letters of this unit were 2I. This version of Spitfire usually flew with clipped wings but, as can be seen from this photograph, some aircraft were fitted with standard wing tips. Amongst the last RCAF fighter squadrons to come to Europe, No 443 Sqn flew its first offensive sorties as part of No 144 Wg just prior to D-Day. Equipped with Mk IXs from March 1944, and then Mk XVIEs from January 1945, the unit scored 36 victories during its push through occupied Europe *(Public Archives of Canada)*

a Merlin 66 manufactured under licence in the US by Packard. Apart from the engine, the Mks LF IX and XVI were almost identical, and there was little difference in performance. The Packard engine was manufactured to American measurements, however, which made it different enough from its Rolls-Royce counterpart to require separate servicing tools and spare parts.

To prevent confusion between the two versions it was decided to allocate a new mark number to the Packard engined version, and it duly became the Mk XVI. Most Mk XVIs were fitted with the 'E' type wing and armament, and later production aircraft were fitted with the distinctive P-51D-inspired cut-back rear fuselage and bubble canopy, which at last improved the pilot's view of his all-important rear hemisphere.

Mk XVIs started to come off the production line at Castle Bromwich in quantity in October 1944. At the beginning of December No 403 Sqn based at Evere near Brussels was the first unit to exchange its Mk IXs for Mk XVIs. Other Mk IX units in the 2nd Tactical Air Force quickly followed, and by the time the war in Europe had ended, a total of 19 units had re-equipped with this version.

Because of the need for separate servicing tools and spare parts for the Packard engines, squadrons quickly made the change from the Mk IX to the Mk XVI, and it was rare for them to operate both variants simultaneously. By this stage of the war the Griffon-powered Mk XIV had become the primary air superiority version of the Spitfire operating over north-west Europe. As a result the Mk XVI flew mainly in the extremely hazardous fighter-bomber role during the final months of the conflict in Europe.

ENTER THE GRIFFON-ENGINED SPITFIRE

Shortly before the outbreak off war Rolls-Royce engineers began work on a completely new type of aero engine called the Griffon, which was based on the 36.75 litre Rolls-Royce 'R' sprint engine that had powered the Supermarine Schneider Trophy racing seaplanes of a decade earlier. With a cubic capacity one-third greater than of the Merlin, the Griffon II with a single stage supercharger developed 1735 horsepower for take-off. Through inspired juggling with the ancillary components, the designers managed to keep the frontal area of the new engine to within six per cent, its length to within three inches and its weight to within 600 lbs of the equivalent figures for the Merlin. It was immediately evident that the Spitfire could be modified to take the more powerful engine and the prototype Griffon-powered fighter, designated a Mk IV, flew for the first time in November 1941. Soon afterwards there was an attempt to rationalise the growing profusion of Spitfire mark numbers, and the Griffon Spitfire was re-designated as the Mk XX. Then, in April 1942, the designation of the Griffon-powered prototype was again changed and it became the Mk XII.

With the 1735 horsepower delivered from the Griffon II engine through its single-stage two-speed supercharger, the new variant could attain a maximum speed of 372 mph at 5700 ft, a figure that increased to 397 mph at 18,000 ft. As the Griffon Spitfire was undergoing its flight trials, Messerschmitt Bf 109 and Focke-Wulf Fw 190 fighter-bombers were

The prototype Griffon-powered Spitfire, DP845, is seen here on an early proving flight in the spring of 1942. One of two basic Mk IIA airframes ordered in 1941 specially for Rolls-Royce, this machine was structurally 'beefed up' to allow it to harness the vastly increased torque forces associated with the Griffon powerplant. Progressively designated a Mk IV, Mk XX and finally a Mk XII, this machine was ultimately modified to represent a full production standard Mk XII, and boasted clipped wings and cannon armament. This variant was the only member of the burgeoning Spitfire family to be fitted with a single-stage supercharged Griffon, hence the circular oil cooler fitted under the port wing of this fighter

mounting an increasing number of 'tip and run' attacks against targets on the English coast. The raiders ran in at low altitude to avoid radar detection and give the defenders little time to react, so that by the time RAF fighters arrived over the target area the bandits were usually well clear.

To counter the new threat the RAF issued a requirement for an fighter optimised for the low altitude interceptor role. The Spitfire Mk XII was selected and Supermarine received an order to build 100 aircraft. As in the case of the Mk IX, the early production Mk XIIs were essentially Mk Vs with the minimum of modification necessary to enable them to take the more powerful engine. The final batches were Mk VIIIs modified to take the Griffon. All production Mk XIIs had clipped wings to give increased speed at low altitude and a greater rate of roll at all altitudes. Compared with the Mk IX, the Mk XII was 14 mph faster at sea level and 8 mph faster at 10,000 ft; as altitude was increased above 20,000 ft, however, the Mk XII became progressively slower than the Mk IX.

THE MK XII IN SERVICE

In February 1943 No 41 Sqn moved to High Ercal in Shropshire to exchange its Spitfire Vs for Mk XIIs. So far as Spitfire pilots were concerned, the main difference in handling the Griffon-powered Spitfires was that the latter's engine rotated in the opposite direction to the Merlin. Thus, instead of a tendency to swing to the left on take-off, the new version swung rather more strongly to the right. Provided a pilot was aware of the difference and applied sufficient rudder trim to counteract for the swing before it developed, the take off was normal. Sqn Ldr Tom Neil, commander of the unit, latter commented: ·

'As the Mark XII was reputedly faster than the Typhoon low down it was regarded as something of a "hot ship", and there was a painful

Spitfire Mk XII MB858 of No 41 Sqn, based at Westhampnett in late 1943. Part of the second batch of production Mk XIIs built by Vickers-Armstrongs to an order placed in May 1942, this aircraft first flew in July 1943, and was issued to No 41 Sqn two months later

The final production Mk XII, MB882, is seen here being flown by Flt Lt Donald Smith of No 41 Sqn up from Friston in April 1944 – the aircraft bore the identification letters EB-B. Born in South Australia and trained to fly by the RAAF, Smith saw combat over Malta with No 126 Sqn in Spitfire Mk VCs in 1942, had a spell with No 41 Sqn as a flight commander on Mk XIIs and finished up commanding No 453 Sqn, RAAF, on Spitfire Mk IXs over the D-Day beaches. His victory score eventually totalled five aircraft destroyed and one shared destroyed, two probably destroyed and two damaged

air of smugness abroad at dispersal. Our collective ego, however, was knocked sideways when the first XII was delivered by a pretty, pink-cheeked young thing in ATA (Air Transport Auxiliary) uniform, who taxied in with a flourish and stepped out as though she had been flying nothing more vicious than a Tiger Moth. The remainder, all delivered by the fair sex, came in ones and twos until we had a full complement of 18.'

No 41 Sqn became operational in April 1943 and moved to Hawkinge near Folkestone. The unit flew standing patrols trying to intercept enemy fighter-bombers attacking coastal targets, but initially these defensive operations had no success. The Spitfire Mk XII fired its guns in anger for the first time on the 17th of that month, when Flg Off C Birbeck strafed an enemy patrol boat. Later that day Flt Lt R Hogarth shot down a Junkers Ju 88 near Calais.

Initially Mk XIIs had few encounters with enemy aircraft but, as Tom Neil explained, that did not mean their sorties were devoid of excitement:

'One of our early problems was to convince the Typhoons at Lympne and Manston that we were on their side. Our clipped wings gave us the appearance of '109s and there were several ugly encounters between the Typhoons and ourselves, with us on the receiving end. Fortunately, we could just outdistance a Typhoon provided we saw it in time, otherwise blood would have been spilled.'

In April the second and final unit to receive the new version, No 91 Sqn, began its conversion. Commanded by the fighter ace Sqn Ldr Raymond Harries, the squadron joined its sister unit at Hawkinge in May and began operations. The new unit was the first to demonstrate the

Cruising over the West Country whilst up on a virtually full squadron-strength patrol from their Bolt Head base in Devon, elements of No 41 Sqn format loosely on the camera-ship, with Flt Lt Donald Smith closest to the photographer in the familiar MB882. All seven of these aircraft exhibit signs of hard use at low-level out over the Channel, paint scuffing and chipping around the wing roots and engine cowlings denoting rigorous maintenance schedule between sweeps. By this stage in No 41 Sqn's war, the threat posed by low-level coastal raiders was rapidly diminishing, as the handful of Fighter Command squadrons dotted along the south coast dedicated to repelling these nuisance attacks had fairly blunted the Luftwaffe attacks the previous autumn
(via Jerry Scutts)

Spitfire Mk XIVs of No 130 Sqn, photographed shortly after the unit had moved to Duerne, in Belgium, in October 1944. From the squadron's inception in June 1941 until the arrival of the Mk XIVs in August 1944, No 130 Sqn flew Spitfire Mk VB and Cs from various stations across the UK. Despatched to Belgium at the end of September 1944 as part of 2 TAF, the unit enjoyed considerable success with the Mk XIV Spit, claiming 59 German aircraft shot down and 11^{1}/$_{2}$ V1s destroyed *(IWM)*

The most publicised of all Spitfire Mk XIV units was No 610 'County of Chester' Sqn, who took delivery of their first Griffon-engined aircraft on 6 January 1944. Heavily covered by the press at the time, a series of aerial shots were taken in the weeks after the Spitfires had arrived in Exeter. Initially part of the Culmhead Wing, the unit moved east to West Malling in mid-June to help combat the V1 menace – it claimed 50 'Divers' shot down *(via Jerry Scutts)*

effectiveness of the Mk XII in the low-level interception role when, on the evening of 25 May, six of its pilots engaged a force of enemy Fw 190 fighter-bombers attacking Folkestone. In the running combat that followed the Spitfires claimed six enemy aircraft destroyed, two of them falling to Harris's guns.

Although the Spitfire Mk XII was faster than its opponents at low and medium altitudes, when it took part in offensive sweeps its pilots found difficulty in exploiting their advantage because German pilots showed an understandable reluctance to be drawn into fights with Spitfires of any type below 20,000 ft.

In August Raymond Harries was promoted to Wing Commander and was appointed leader of the Wing comprising the two Spitfire Mk XII squadrons. By that time his confirmed victory total stood at 10^{3}/$_{4}$, of which 5^{1}/$_{2}$ were scored while flying Griffon-engined Spitfires. Sqn Ldr Norman Kynaston replaced Harries as commander of No 91 Sqn, and duly enjoyed similar successes with the Mk XII, particularly against the V1 threat in mid-1944.

The Mk XII Wing fought its most successful operation on 20 October 1943, when the two squadrons mounted a fighter sweep over northern France. Near Rouen about 25 Bf 109Gs and Fw 190s dived on the Spitfires from out of the sun. The RAF pilots turned to face their attackers head-on, however, and for once the German fighters stayed to fight. In the mêlée that followed the Mk XII pilots claimed the destruction of eight enemy fighters, without loss to themselves.

THE MK XIV
IN SERVICE

As previously stated, the Mk XII was essentially a Mk V or a Mk VIII with the minimum of modification necessary to enable it to take the early version of the Griffon engine with single-stage supercharging. The definitive Griffon-powered version of the Spitfire, with a two-stage supercharger and redesigned and strengthened wing, was the Mk

31

21, but this variant would not be ready for service until the war in Europe was almost over. As a stop-gap the Mk XIV was placed in production, being essentially a Mk VIII fitted with the Griffon 65 engine that boasted a two-stage supercharger that developed 1540 hp for take-off and 2035 hp at 7000 ft. The new version gave a considerable improvement in performance compared with the Mk IX.

The first squadron to receive the Mk XIV was No 610, based at Exeter, in January 1944. During March Nos 91 and 322 Sqns also began converting to the new version. All three units were fully operational in June, when the V1 flying bomb attack on London commenced.

As in the case of the Mk XII, the Griffon engine fitted in the Spitfire Mk XIV rotated in the opposite direction to that in a Merlin-powered Spitfire. Pilots were all supposed to be briefed on this difference before their first flight, but sometimes the system fell down. Fighter ace Wg Cdr Robert Oxspring, commanding the Manston Wing in 1944, told the author of one such instance:

A late-production Spitfire FR XIV fitted with a bubble canopy. The circular window for the sideways-looking oblique camera may be seen just forward of the fuselage roundel. This aircraft belonged to No 268 Sqn, a dedicated fighter-reconnaissance unit which operated from Twente, in Holland, during the final weeks of the war *(Houston)*

Spitfire Mk XIVs of No 132 Sqn on the flightdeck of the escort carrier HMS *Smiter*, which transported the unit from India to Hong Kong in September 1945 following the Japanese surrender – no combat was seen by the unit with the Mk XiVs *(via Aeroplane)*

'We had an Australian pilot at Manston who had been shot down over France, and after many adventures he had managed to get back via Spain. He did not bother to tell the authorities about it, and just rolled up at the squadron so we let him fly again. In the meantime we had re-equipped from Spitfire IXs to Mark XIVs, and not only did the XIV had a much greater engine torque but the propeller went round in the opposite direction. Well, you can imagine the problems.

'He wound on the rudder trim in the wrong direction and opened the throttle. When the five-bladed prop bit, the aircraft swung round sharply and went bounding over the grass in a curve. When he eventually he got off the ground he was going at about 90 degrees to the runway, and he narrowly missed the line of hangars. It scared the life out of him! In the end he got the Spitfire down all right, but he was very subdued for the next week or so.'

In September 1944 Allied ground forces over-ran the last V1 launching sites in the Pas de Calais area, and the initial phase of the bombardment came to an end. That freed the three squadrons of Mk XIVs to move to Belgian, where they were soon joined by four more that had re-equipped with this variant; Nos 41, 130, 350 and 402 Sqns. From then until the end of the war the Mk XIV was the main air superiority fighter operated by the 2nd Tactical Air Force in northern Europe. Later, production versions were fitted with the `E' type wing and 20 mm cannon armament, and improved visibility bubble canopies.

Also in the autumn of 1944 a fighter-reconnaissance version appeared – the FR XIV. This carried a single F.24 oblique camera in the rear fuselage pointing either to port or starboard, and an additional tank in the rear fuselage containing 33 gallons of fuel. Nos 2 and 430 Sqns re-equipped with this variant in November 1944.

In June 1945 the first Spitfire Mk XIVs arrived in India, and during August two squadrons, Nos 11 and 17, were declared operational with this variant. The war came to an end before the Mk XIV could see action, however, but there was still work for it to do. Following the Japanese surrender the two squadron's aircraft were craned aboard the aircraft carrier HMS *Trumpeter*, which transported them to within range of Singapore. The fighters then gingerly took off from her deck to land a short time later at the recently liberated Seletar airfield on Singapore island, where they formed an integral part of the occupation force.

Top and above **Spitfire Mk XIV RN135 was the personal mount of Sqn Ldr James 'Ginger' Lacey, commander of No 17 Sqn based at Seletar, Singapore, in the autumn of 1945. At the end of the war his victory score stood at 28 enemy aircraft destroyed, 5 probably destroyed and 9 damaged, but only one of these kills was achieved while flying a late-mark Spitfire – on 19 February 1945 he downed a Ki 43 'Oscar' 30 miles south of Mandalay whilst leading a patrol of No 17 Sqn Spitfire Mk VIIIs from Ywadon, in Burma** *(N Wilkinson via Geoff Thomas)*

COLOUR PLATES

This 18-page section profiles many of the aircraft flown by late-mark Spitfire aces of World War 2. The majority of these aircraft have never been seen in colour before, and the shear breadth of variation in unit markings and camouflage schemes is quite fascinating. As is always the case in this ever-growing series, the artworks have all been specially commissioned for this volume, and profile artists Chris Davey, Keith Fretwell and Mark Rolfe, plus figure artist Mike Chappell, have gone to great pains to illustrate the aircraft, and their pilots, as accurately as possible following much original in-depth research.

1
Mk IXC BR369/EH-T of Wg Cdr Eric Thomas, OC Biggin Hill Wing, August 1942

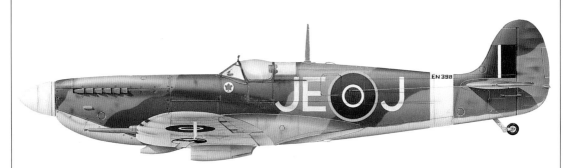

2
Mk IX EN398/JE-J of Wg Cdr 'Johnnie' Johnson, OC Kenley Wing, spring 1943

3
Mk XIV RM787/CG of Wg Cdr Colin Gray, OC flying, Lympne, October 1944

4
F VII MD188/PB of Wg Cdr Peter Brothers, OC Culmhead Wing, June 1944

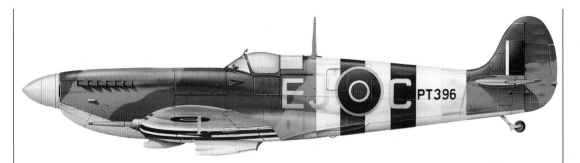

5
LF IX PT396/EJ-C of Wg Cdr 'Jack' Charles RCAF, OC Tangmere Wing, August 1944

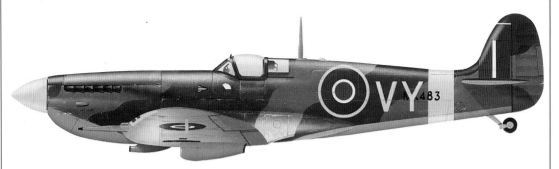

6
LF IX MK483/VY of Wg Cdr Adolphe Vybiral, OC of the Czech-manned North Weald Wing, 1944

7
LF VIII A58-464/CR-C of Grp Capt Clive Caldwell, OC No 80 Wg RAAF, Morotai, summer 1945

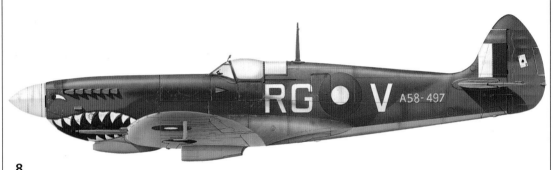

8
LF VIII A58-497/RG-V of Wg Cdr Robert Gibbes, Deputy Wing Leader No 80 Wg RAAF, Sattler Field, Northern Territory, summer 1944

9
LF IX MJ845/HBW of Wg Cdr Harold Bird-Wilson, OC No 122 Wg, Funtington, January 1944

10
Mk XIVE RM809/GCK of Wg Cdr George Clinton Keefer, OC No 125 Wg, Eindhoven, Holland, March 1945

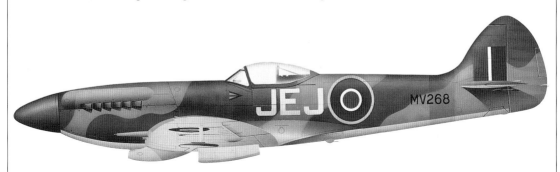

11
Mk XIVE MV268/JEJ of Grp Capt 'Johnnie' Johnson, OC No 127 Wg, 2 TAF, Soltau, Germany, May 1945

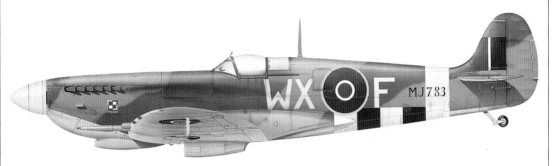

12
LF IXC MJ783/WX-F of Grp Capt Aleksander Gabszewicz, OC No 131 Wg, 2 TAF, Lille/Vendeville, France, September 1944

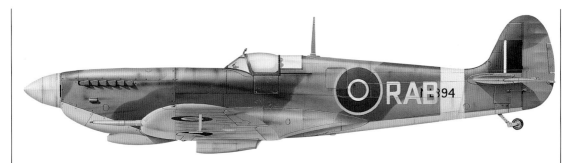

13
LF IX ML294/RAB, of Wg Cdr Rolfe Berg, OC No 132 Wg, 2 TAF, Grimbergen, Belgium, December 1944

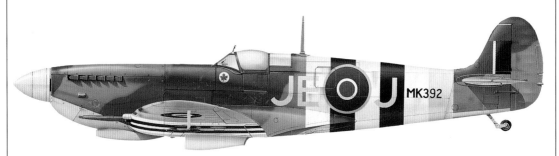

14
LF IX MK392 JE-J of Wg Cdr 'Johnnie' Johnson, OC No 144 Wg, Ford, June 1944

15
Mk VIII MD371/FB of Grp Capt Robert Boyd, OC No 239 Wg, Baigachi, India, 1944

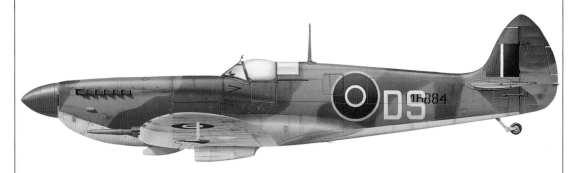

16
LF IX MH884/DS of Grp Capt Wilfred Duncan-Smith, OC No 324 Wg, Calvi, Corsica, August 1944

17
Mk XIV RN135/YB-A of Sqn Ldr 'Ginger' Lacey, OC No 17 Sqn, Seletar, Singapore, autumn 1945

18
Mk XII EN237/EB-V of Sqn Ldr Thomas Neil, OC No 41 Sqn, Hawkinge, spring 1943

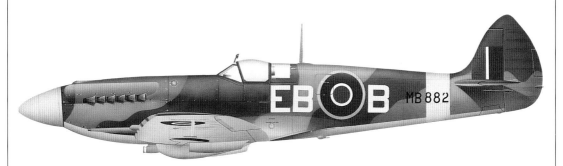

19
Mk XII MB882/EB-B of Flt Lt Donald Smith of No 41 Sqn, Friston, April 1944

20
Mk XIVE MV266/EB-J of Sqn Ldr John Shepherd, OC No 41 Sqn, Twente, Holland, April 1945

21
Mk IXC BR600/V-SH of Plt Off Donald Kingaby of No 64 Sqn, Hornchurch, July 1942

22
Mk IXC BR581/Z-SH of Sqn Ldr Wilfred Duncan-Smith, OC of No 64 Sqn, Hornchurch, August 1942

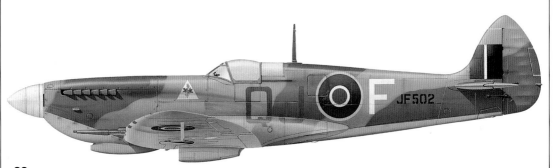

23
F VIII JF502/QJ-F of Flt Lt 'Eddie' Edwards of No 92 Sqn, Marcianise, Italy, early 1944

24
Mk IX MH934/HN-C of Wt Off Bobby Bunting of No 93 Sqn, Lago, Italy, in February 1944

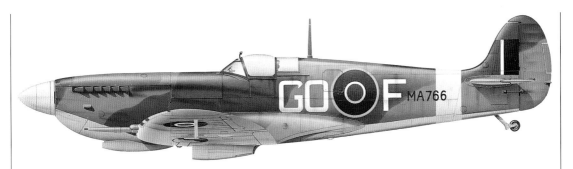

25
Mk IX MA766/GO-F of Sqn Ldr Russell Foskett, OC No 94 Sqn, LG147/Bu Amud, Cyrenaica, June 1944

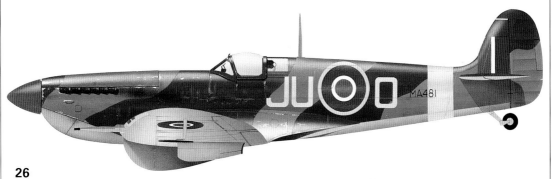

26
Mk IX MA481/JU-O of Flg Off Irving 'Hap' Kennedy of No 111 Sqn, Falcone, Sicily, September 1943

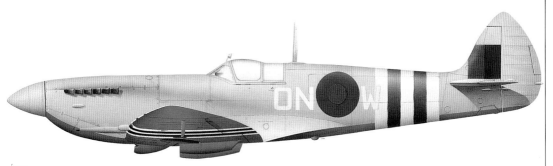

27
F VII MD139/ON-W of Flg Off Walter Hibbert of No 124 Sqn, Bradwell Bay, June 1944

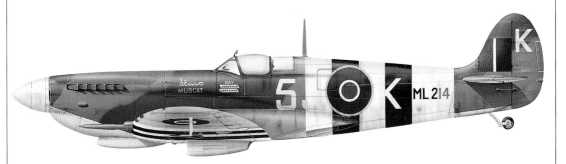

28
LF IX ML214/5J-K of Sqn Ldr John Plagis, OC No 126 Sqn, Culmhead, July 1944

29
Mk IX MA621/DV-A of Flt Lt F 'Tony' Gaze of No 129 Sqn, Hornchurch, August 1943

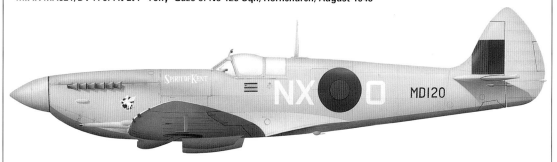

30
F VII MD120/NX-O of Sqn Ldr James O'Meara, OC No 131 Sqn, Colerne, March 1944

31
Mk XIVE RN133/FF-B of Sqn Ldr Kenneth Charney, OC No 132 Sqn, Madura, India, August 1945

32
Mk IX EN459/ZX-1 of Flt Lt Eugeniusz Horbaczewski of the Polish Fighting Team, attached to No 145 Sqn, Tunisia, in the spring of 1943

33
Mk IX EN315/ZX-6 of Sqn Ldr Stanislaw Skalski, OC of the Polish Fighting Team attached to No 145
Sqn, Tunisia, spring 1943

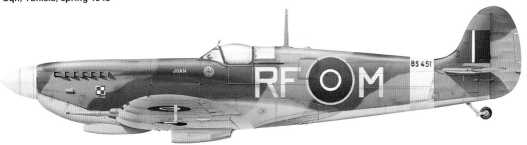

34
Mk IXC BS451/RF-M of Sqn Ldr Jan Falkowski, OC No 303 Sqn, Northolt, June 1943

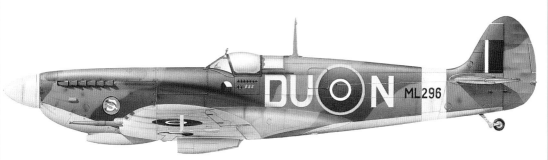

35
HF IX ML296/DU-N of Flt Lt Otto Smik of No 312 Sqn, Lympne, September 1944

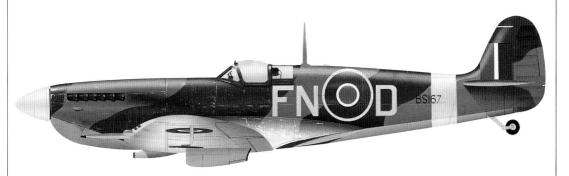

36
Mk IX BS167/FN-D of Flt Lt Ragnar Dogger of No 331 Sqn, North Weald, July 1943

37
Mk IXC BS248/AH-O of Sgt Ola Aanjesen of No 332 Sqn, North Weald, summer 1943

38
Mk IX BS393/GW-Z of Lt Michel Boudier of No 340 Sqn, Biggin Hill, October 1942

39
Mk IX BS538/NL-B of Sgt Pierre Clostermann of No 341 Sqn, Biggin Hill, June 1943

40
Mk XIVE SM825/MN-M of Sqn Ldr Harold Walmsley, OC No 350 Sqn, Celle, Germany, April 1945

41
FR XIVE RM785/T of Sqn Ldr William Klersy, OC No 401 Sqn, Wunstorf, Germany, May 1945

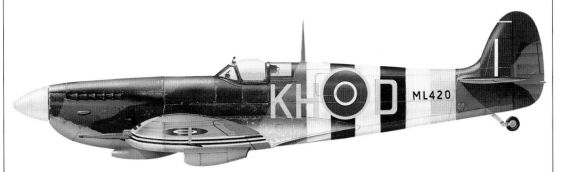

42
LF IX ML420/KH-D of Flt Lt James Lindsay of No 403 Sqn, Tangmere, June 1944

43
LF IXE RR201/DB-A of Flt Lt Dick Audet of No 411 Sqn, Heesch, Holland, December 1944

44
Mk VIII JF469/AN-M of Flt Lt Albert Houle of No 417 Sqn, Gioia del Colle, Italy, October 1943

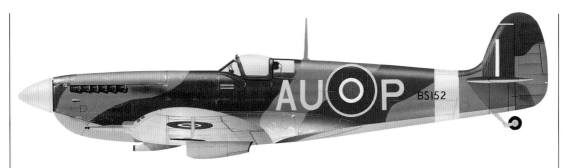

45
Mk IX BS152/AU-P of Sqn Ldr Robert McNair OC No 421 Sqn, Kenley, June 1943

46
LF IX MK399/9G-K of Flt Lit Frederick Wilson of No 441 Sqn, Westhampnett, May 1944

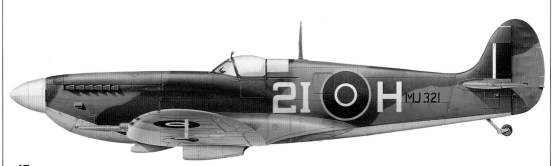

47
Mk IX MK321/2I-H of Sqn Ldr Henry McLeod, OC No 443 Sqn, Westhampnett, April 1944

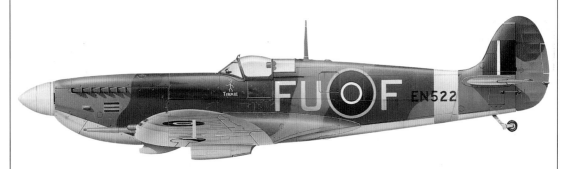

48
Mk IX EN522/FU-F of Sqn Ldr John Ratten, OC No 453 Sqn, Hornchurch, April 1943

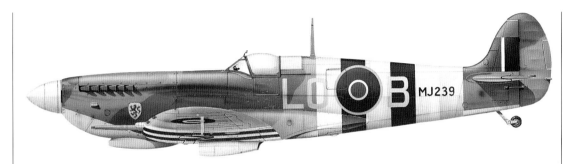

49
LF IX MJ239/LO-B of Flt Lt Kenneth Charney of No 602 Sqn, Longues, Normandy, July 1944

50
LF VIII JG559/AF-N of Flt Lt Wilfred Goold of No 607 Sqn, Imphal, May 1944

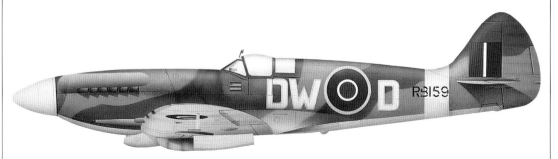

51
Mk XIV RB159/DW-D of Sqn Ldr R Newbery, OC No 610 Sqn, West Malling, 1944

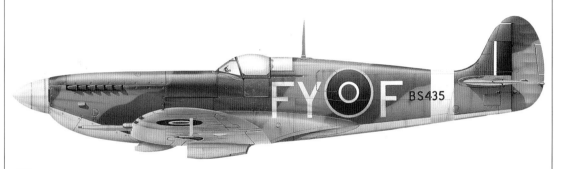

52
Mk IX BS435/FY-F of Sqn Ldr Hugo Armstrong, OC No 611 Sqn, Biggin Hill, February 1942

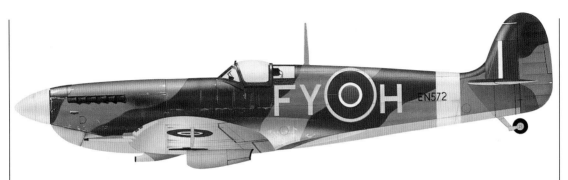

53
LF IX EN572/FY-H of Flt Lt John Checketts of No 611 Sqn, Biggin Hill, May 1943

54
Mk IX MA419/N-V of Flt Lt Warren Schrader of No 1435 Sqn, Brindisi, Italy, December 1943

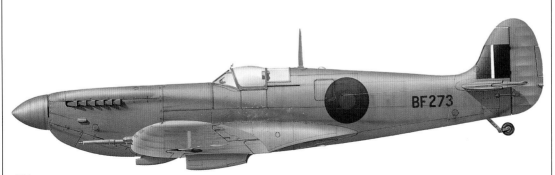

55
Mk IX BF273 of Flg Off Emanuel Galitzine of the High Altitude Flight, Northolt, September 1942

56
Mk VIII CM-M of Lt Col Charles 'Sandy' McCorkle, OC 31st FG, US 12th Air Force, Castel Volturno, Italy, January 1944

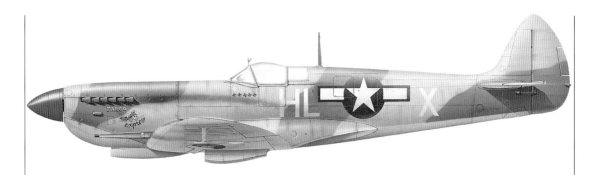

57
Mk VIII HL-X of Lt Leland Molland, 308th FS, 31st FG, US 12 Air Force, Castel Volturno, Italy, January 1944

58
F VIII JF626/AX-W of Maj Henry Gaynor, No 1 Sqn SAAF, Italy, December 1943

1
Wg Cdr Peter Brothers served as OC Culmhead Wing in mid-1944, controlling three Spitfire units

2
Sqn Ldr 'Jack' Charles, RCAF, led No 611 Sqn for six action-packed months at Biggin Hill in mid-1943

3
Flt Lt Henry Zary served as a flight commander with No 421 Sqn in 1943/44, scoring four kills

4
Capt Ragnar Dogger was a flight
commander during his second tour
with No 331 Sqn in 1944/45

5
Wg Cdr 'Johnnie' Johnson led No
144 Wg in support of the D-Day landings, claiming seven kills in 18 days

6
Top-scoring Kiwi ace Sqn Ldr Colin
Gray is seen in desert fatigues whilst
OC of No 81 Sqn in spring 1943

RAMRODS, RODEOS, ROADSTEADS, RHUBARBS AND CIRCUSES

From the beginning of 1941, RAF Fighter Command and later the 2nd Tactical Air Force flew offensive air operations over western Europe code-named as follows:

Ramrod – Attack by bombers (or fighter-bombers) escorted by fighters. The primary object of the operation was the destruction of the target, and the primary role of the fighters was to protect the bombers from fighter attack.

Rodeo – Fighter sweep over enemy territory with no bombers.

Roadstead – Attack on enemy ships at sea by bombers (or fighter/bombers) escorted by fighters.

Rhubarb – Small-scale attack by fighters using cloud cover and surprise, with the object of destroying enemy aircraft in the air and/or striking at ground targets.

Circus– Attack by a small force of bombers with powerful fighter escort, intended to lure enemy fighters into the air so they could be engaged by RAF fighters. The primary objects of the operation were the destruction of enemy fighters and the protection of the bombers from fighter attack.

During 1941 and 1942 the RAF had possessed only small numbers of light and medium bombers suitable for daylight attacks. Initially the Circus operation – an attack by nine or a dozen Blenheim bombers with a heavy fighter escort – was the main type of operation flown by Fighter Command's day fighter squadrons.

By the summer of 1943, however, the emphasis shifted to the Ramrod and Rodeo types of operation. By then the US Army Air Forces had established a large contingent of medium and heavy

Sqn Ldr John Plagis, commander of No 126 'Persian Gulf' Sqn from June to December 1944 introduces an anonymous lady VIP to members of his unit at Bradwell Bay in September 1944. The Mk IX Spitfires in the background were amongst the six aircraft purchased by the Persian Gulf Spitfire Fund, all of which bore the names of states in that area. A Rhodesian of Greek parentage, Plagis flew Spitfire Mk Vs over Malta with Nos 249 and 185 Sqns, before returning to the UK and No 64 Sqn. By the end of the war his victory score stood at 15 enemy aircraft destroyed and two shared destroyed, two shared probably destroyed, six damaged and one shared damaged

bomber units in England, and No 2 Grp of Bomber Command had several squadrons of Mitchells and Bostons. With powerful Spitfire escort, these bombers delivered destructive attacks by day on targets in occupied Europe. On other occasions fighters flew sweeps over enemy territory to enforce air superiority over the area. From then on the Circus and Rhubarb operations saw relatively little use, and the Roadstead went the same way as Coastal Command took over the task of mounting anti-shipping strikes.

To show how elaborate the Ramrod operations had become by the summer of 1943, we shall examine one of these in some detail. Ramrod S.36 took place on the afternoon of 6 September and comprised simultaneous attacks on three railway marshalling yards in northern France.

All three attacks took place at around 1730 hours. The first, by 72 B-26 Marauders, was on the yards at Serqueux. The second, by a similar force of Marauders, was on the yards at Amiens. The third, by 18 Mitchells of the RAF, was on the yards at Abbeville. No fewer than 32 squadrons of Spitfires provided direct support for the attacks.

In addition two squadrons of Spitfire Mk IXs provided general area cover, with an offensive sweep to Arras to block the path of enemy fighters moving from airfields in north-eastern France and Belgium to intercept the bombers. Each of the two Marauder raiding forces had 12 squadrons of Spitfires allocated to its protection, divided as follows:

Close Escort Wing – This comprised five squadrons of Spitfire Vs, its role being to protect the bombers and remain with them throughout the penetration and withdrawal phases of the operation. One squadron was to remain close to the bombers under all circumstances. A second squadron positioned in the vicinity of the bombers, was free to engage enemy fighters attacking the bombers. Two more squadrons provided top cover for the escort Wing, though they were permitted to come down to engage the enemy. A fifth squadron was positioned about 1000 ft below and behind the bomber formation, to block the path of enemy fighters attempting to dive beneath the bombers and attack them in a zoom climb.

Escort Cover Wing – This comprised two squadrons of Spitfire Mk Vs, and they had to protect both the bombers and the Escort Wing. These fighters flew up-sun of the formation and had greater freedom of action than the Escort Wing, but they still had to remain near to the bombers.

High Cover Wing – This comprised two squadrons of Spitfire Mk IXs, and its role was to protect the Escort Cover Wing. These fighters had greater freedom of action than the other two Wings, and they normally flew up-sun of the Escort Cover Wing with the two squadrons stepped up towards the sun. The lower squadron was free to engage the enemy at any time, while the higher squadron remained in position for as long as possible.

Top Cover Wing – This comprised three squadrons of Spitfire Mk IXs in the case of the Serqueux attack force, or two squadrons of Mk IXs and four Mk VIIs in the case of the Amiens attack force.

The smaller force of RAF Mitchells attacking Abbeville required a smaller escort than the large formations of Marauders – its Close Escort Wing comprised only two units of Mk Vs, with the Escort Cover Wing similarly constituted and the High Cover Wing boasting two squadrons of Mk IXs.

Flt Lt Stanislaw Blok of No 315 'City of Deblin' Sqn, seen with his damaged Mk IX Spitfire at Northolt following a brush with Fw 190s over France. His final score stood at five aircraft destroyed, one probably destroyed and two or three damaged *(Dr Koniarek Archives)*

Flt Lt Henryk Pietrzak of No 306 'City of Torun' Sqn, pictured on 31 December 1942 after landing his Spitfire Mk IX at Northolt following a mission over France during which he shot down an Fw 190 – his was the 500th aerial victory credited to the Polish units based in the United Kingdom. At the end of the war his score stood at seven aircraft destroyed and two shared, two damaged and four, and one shared, V1s destroyed *(Dr Koniarek Archives)*

Usually German fighter force based in north-west Europe avoided stand-up fights with the powerful Ramrod attack formations, but on this occasion the defenders reacted forcefully. All three of the raiding forces taking part in Ramrod S.36 were engaged by German fighters.

The High Cover Wing of the Serqueux raiding force, comprising Spitfire Mk IXs of Nos 341 and 485 Sqns, came under determined attack as the bombers turned away from the target. No 341 Sqn was jumped by about 20 Bf 109s, while No 485 became embroiled with a similar number of Fw 190s. Sqn Ldr John Checketts, commander of No 485 Sqn, led his section down to engage and they found themselves alone with about 12 Bf 109s. As a result of combat one Bf 109G was claimed destroyed and one Fw 190 damaged, but Checketts himself was shot down and parachuted to safety – picked up by the French resistance soon after he landed, the New Zealander would be back in England within seven weeks.

The Escort Cover Wing of the Amiens attack force fought a brisk skirmish with about a dozen Bf 109s in the target area and a Spitfire Mk V pilot of No 317 Sqn claimed one of the German fighters shot down. At about the same time No 129 Sqn – part of the High Cover Wing – also came under attack. One of its Mk IXs collided with, or was rammed by, an Fw 190 and both aircraft were destroyed.

While this was happening the Top Cover Wing, comprising Spitfire Mk IXs of Nos 303 and 316 Sqns, and a few Mk VIIs of No 124 Sqn, engaged another formation of enemy fighters. Sqn Ldr Jan Falkowski, commander of No 303 Sqn, claimed his ninth aerial victory that day:

'The squadron making a right turn east of Amiens saw about eight '109s flying behind the main formation and 6 - 8 Fw 190s in pairs approaching the target area from SW. All EA flying at about 25,000 ft. I dived to attack with my squadron from about 28/29000 ft and approached the first pair of Fw 190s to about 500 yds, then I gave two long bursts closing range to 300 yds. After second burst enemy aircraft started smoking with black smoke. In that time I noticed flashes of tracer passing by my cockpit and when I pulled up another Fw 190 passed by my Spitfire. After I turned to the left I saw about 5000 ft below me a Fw 190 in flames, and about one mile to the south another smoking Fw 190.'

Four other Poles also made victory claims – Flt Lt Wandizlak, Plt Off Sliwinski and Flt Sgt Chudek each claimed an Fw 190, and Sgt Czezowski claimed a Bf 109.

The High Cover Wing of the Abbeville raiding force, comprising Spitfire IXs of Nos 403 and 421 Sqns, also came under attack near the target. Flt Lt Southwood and Flg Off Dowding of No 403 Sqn each claimed an Fw 190 destroyed, and pilots of No 421 Sqn claimed one of these aircraft damaged.

In each case the bombers completed their attacks without interference, and afterwards withdrew without loss. The protective fighter sweep to Arras, flown by Spitfire Mk IXs of Nos 331 and 332 Sqns, passed off without incident.

A later production Spitfire Mk IX (note the broad chord rudder) of No 313 'Czech' Sqn. A small Czech roundel has been stencilled onto the fuselage underneath the cockpit, and an unidentifiable personal insignia adorns the staboard engine cowling. This aircraft is also fitted with a 'slipper' tank *(via Jerry Scutts)*

THE LEADING ACES

Note: the ten top-scoring aces who flew late mark Spitfires are listed below in order of their total victory scores. The headline rank was that held at end of World War 2.

GRP CAPT
JAMES EDGAR 'JOHNNIE' JOHNSON

Born in Barrow upon Soar in Leicestershire, Johnson joined the RAF shortly after the outbreak of war. He first went into action with No 616 Sqn in December 1940 flying Spitfire Mk Is. Early in 1941 the unit re-equipped with Mk IIAs, and a few months later Mk Vs arrived. During fighter sweeps over occupied Europe he gained his first combat experience and achieved his first confirmed victory, a Bf 109E shot down over northern France on 26 June 1941 whilst flying A Spitfire Mk IIA. On several occasions he flew as wingman for Wg Cdr Douglas Bader.

In June 1942, when his victory score stood at seven enemy aircraft destroyed, and one shared, he was promoted to Squadron Leader and took command of No 610 Sqn with Spitfire Mk Vs. In March 1943 he was promoted to Wing Commander and took command of the Canadian-manned Kenley Wing, equipped with Spitfire Mk IXs. During the next six months he claimed a further 14 victories, plus shares in a further five kills – for this success he was awarded the DSO. In September 1943 Johnson began a 'rest' tour, and was appointed to the Planning Staff at headquarters No 11 Grp. In March 1944 he returned to the frontline and was appointed to command another Canadian-manned Wing, No 144, which was also equipped with Mk IXs Spitfires. He led this unit during the Normandy assault, and on into the critical first weeks of the invasion. In August the Wing was disbanded and he moved to take command of No 127 Wg, where he stayed until early 1945. On 6 April 1945 he was promoted to Group Captain and appointed commander of No 127 Wg, which was equipped with Spitfire Mk XIVs. Between then and the end of the conflict he did not add to his score, however.

At the end of the war his victory tally stood at 34 enemy aircraft destroyed (27 while flying the Spitfire Mk IX) and 7 shared destroyed, plus a further 3 and 2 shared probably destroyed, 10 and 3 shared damaged and 1 shared destroyed on the ground. 'Johnnie' Johnson was the top-scoring Spitfire pilot of the war, and he achieved all of his victories while flying this type. Significantly, with the exception of a Bf 110 that was shared, all of his aerial victories were against single-engined fighters.

After the war he continued in the RAF and reached the rank of Air Vice-Marshal.

SQN LDR NEVILLE DUKE

Born in Tunbridge, Kent, Neville Duke joined the RAF in June 1940. He commenced operations in April 1941 when he was posted to No 92 Sqn, who were then flying offensive sweeps with Spitfire Mk Vs over occupied Europe. On several occasions he flew as wingman to Wg Cdr `Sailor'

Sqn Ldr Neville Duke was the top-scoring RAF pilot in the Mediterranean theatre. During 1944 he commanded No 145 Sqn with Spitfire Mk VIIIs, and at the end of the war his victory total stood at 26 enemy aircraft destroyed and 2 shared destroyed, 1 probably destroyed, 6 damaged and 2 shared destroyed on the ground and 1 shared probably destroyed on the ground. Duke is seen here earlier in the war when he flew Spitfire Mk Vs *(via Shores)*

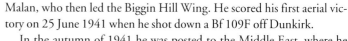

Malan, who then led the Biggin Hill Wing. He scored his first aerial victory on 25 June 1941 when he shot down a Bf 109F off Dunkirk.

In the autumn of 1941 he was posted to the Middle East, where he joined No 112 Sqn flying Tomahawks and later Kittyhawks. From then on his score built up rapidly, and by the end of February 1942 it stood at a total of eight confirmed and three probable victories.

In April 1942 Duke was posted to the Fighter School at El Ballal in Egypt as an instructor. In the following November he rejoined his old squadron, No 92, which by then had moved to Tunisia with its Spitfire Mk Vs. Duke became a flight commander with the unit, his score mounting to the extent that in March 1943 he was awarded the DSO.

In June 1943 his second operational tour came to an end and he was promoted to Squadron Leader and posted to No 73 Operational Training Unit at Abu Sueir, in Egypt, as Chief Flying Instructor. In March 1944 he was appointed commander of No 145 Sqn in Italy, flying Spitfire Mk VIIIs. In the following September that tour came to an end and he was posted back to England. His victory total now stood at 26 aircraft destroyed (8 while flying Spitfire Mk VIIIs or IXs) and 2 shared destroyed, 1 probably destroyed, 6 damaged and 2 shared destroyed on the ground and 1 shared probably destroyed on the ground. That made Duke the top-scoring RAF.pilot in the Mediterranean theatre.

In January 1945 he became a production test pilot with the Hawker Aircraft Company. After completing the course at the Empire Test Pilot's School at Cranfield he joined the RAF High Speed Flight in June 1946,before being posted onto the staff of the Aircraft and Armament Experimental Establishment at Boscombe Down early in 1947. In June 1948 he resigned his RAF commission to take up a post as test pilot with Hawker Aircraft Ltd. In 1951 he became Chief Test Pilot, and in this capacity he was responsible for directing the flight test programme for the new Hunter fighter. In 1953, flying a specially modified Hunter, he raised the World Air Speed Record to 727 mph.

WG CDR
COLIN FALKLAND GRAY

Born in Christchurch, New Zealand, Gray joined the RAF in 1938. After completing his flying training he was posted to No 54 Sqn in November 1939, flying Spitfire Mk Is. He first saw action during the operations to cover the Dunkirk evacuation, and his first confirmed victory was a Bf 109 shot down near Gravelines on 25 May 1940. During the intensive air fighting of the next few months he was frequently in action, and by the end of the Battle of Britain his victory score stood at 16 enemy aircraft destroyed and 1 probably destroyed. During 1941 he spent brief periods with Nos 1, 41, 43, 54, 403 and 616 Sqns, adding only two more victories to his tally, before being sent to a headquarters post as a rest tour. In September 1942 he returned to operations flying with Nos 403 and 616 Sqns, before taking command of No 64 Sqn with Spitfire Mk IXs. Gray was then posted to Tunisia and, after a brief spell as a staff officer at headquarters No 333 Grp, he took command of No 81 Sqn then re-equipping with Spitfire Mk IXs. With that unit he added five more victories to his score, and in May 1943 was promoted to Wing Commander. He led No 322 Wg in action during the invasion of Sicily, and the operations that followed. In October 1943 he returned to England to complete another tour as a staff officer. In July 1944 he commanded first the Detling Wing then the Lympne Wing for short periods during operations against the V1 flying bombs.

At the end of the war his victory score stood at 27 aircraft destroyed (7 while flying the Spitfire Mk IX) and 2 shared destroyed, 6 and 4 shared probably destroyed and 12 damaged, making him the top-scoring New Zealand fighter pilot. After the war he continued in the RAF, attaining the rank of Group Captain.

WG CDR LANCE WADE

Born in Texas, USA, Lance Wade joined the RAF in Canada in December 1940. After completing his flying training he went to the Middle East in September 1941, flying a Hurricane off the aircraft carrier HMS *Ark Royal* to Malta, and continuing on to Egypt the following day by flying boat. Once there, he joined No 33 Sqn, who were flying Hurricanes, and gained his first victories on 18 November 1941 when he shot down two Italian CR 42 fighters. When his combat tour ended in September 1942 his victory score stood at 12 enemy aircraft destroyed. He then returned to the USA for a few months, but in January 1943 returned to North Africa and was appointed to No 145 Sqn as a flight commander. Wade assumede command of the unit just months later upon his promotion to Squadron Leader. In March the No 145 Sqn exchanged its Spitfire Mk Vs for Mk IXs, then in the following June it re-equipped with Mk VIIIs. Wade remained in command until November 1943, when he was promoted to Wing Commander and moved to a staff appointment at Headquarters Desert Air Force. In January 1944, during a routine flight in an Auster, the aircraft went into a spin at low altitude and crashed into the ground, killing the fighter ace. At the time of his death Wade's victory score stood at 22 aircraft destroyed (5 while flying Mk VIIIs or IXs) and 2 shared destroyed, 1 probably destroyed and 13 damaged in the air, plus 1 destroyed and 5 damaged on the ground. He was the top-scoring American-born pilot to complete the whole of his combat career in the RAF

SQN LDR
JOHANNES JACOBUS 'CHRIS' LE ROUX

Born in the Transvaal, South Africa, 'Chris' Le Roux joined the RAF in February 1939. His career as a fighter pilot began in February 1941 when he was posted to No 91 Sqn flying Spitfire Mk IIs then Vs. His first aerial victory was on 17 August 1941 when he shot down a Bf 109E near Boulogne. His first tour ended in December 1941 and he spent the next six months first as an instructor at No 55 Operational Training Unit (OTU). Then Le Roux served as a production test pilot with Rolls-Royce Ltd, flying Spitfire Mk Vs modified into Mk IXs through the installation of a Merlin 61 engine. In September 1942 he returned to No 91 Sqn and Spitfire Mk Vs, where he quickly gained further victories. In January 1943 he was posted to Tunisia to command No 111 Sqn with Spitfire Mk Vs and remained with the unit until the end of the fighting in North Africa. After a spell as a fighter controller, Le Roux took command of No

602 Sqn in July 1944, who were equipped with Spitfire Mk IXs. On the 17th of that month during an armed reconnaissance over the Normandy battle area, he strafed a staff car seen moving at speed in the open. With its driver dead at the wheel following the attack, the car ran off the road and crashed into a tree. The passenger in the vehicle was Field Marshal Erwin Rommel, commander of the German ground forces in Normandy, and he duly suffered a fractured skull and severe concussion, and had to be relieved of his command. On 29 August 1944 Le Roux took off from Normandy in bad weather to fly to England, but he was never seen again and was posted missing. At this time his victory score stood at 18 aircraft destroyed (6 while flying Mk IXs), 2 probably destroyed and 8 damaged.

WG CDR
DONALD ERNEST KINGABY

Born in Holloway, London, Donald Kingaby joined the RAF in September 1939. His career as a fighter pilot began in June 1940 when as a Sergeant he was posted to No 266 Sqn, equipped with Spitfire Mk Is. He served with that unit and then No 92 Sqn during the Battle of Britain, and by the end of the year his victory score stood at eight aircraft destroyed. Early in 1941 No 92 Sqn re-equipped with Spitfire Mk Vs and Kingaby's score continued to mount.

In November 1941 he went to No 58 OTU as an instructor, and soon afterwards he received his commission. In March 1942 he was posted to No 111 Sqn, but a month later he moved to No 64 Sqn as a flight commander. He was with the unit when it received the RAF's first Spitfire Mk IXs and, as recounted earlier in this volume, achieved the first victory in this mark when he shot down an Fw 190 off Boulogne on 30 July 1942.

Sqn Ldr Donald Kingaby (sixth from left), the commander of No 122 Sqn, with pilots of his unit at Hornchurch in the winter of 1942/43. Earlier, while flying with No 64 Sqn, he had achieved the first victory in a Spitfire Mk IX when he shot down an Fw 190 off Boulogne on 30 July 1942. At the end of the war his score stood at 21 enemy aircraft destroyed (5 while flying Spitfire Mk IXs) and 2 shared destroyed, 6 probably destroyed and 11 damaged (*via Norman Franks*)

In August Kingaby was posted to No 122 Sqn, a move which was quickly followed by his promotion to the rank of Squadron Leader in November, after which he took command of the unit. In March 1943 he received the DSO, was promoted to Wing Commander and took command of the Hornchurch Wing. In September 1943 Kingaby moved to a staff post at headquarters Fighter Command, from where he was posted to the Advanced Gunnery School at Catfoss – here he remained until the end of the conflict. At the end of the war Kingaby's score stood at 21 enemy aircraft destroyed (5 while flying Spitfire Mk IXs) and 2 shared destroyed, 6 probably destroyed and 11 damaged. After the war he continued in the RAF and eventually attained the rank of Wing Commander.

SQN LDR
HENRY WALLACE MCLEOD

Born in Regina, Canada, McLeod joined the RCAF in September 1940. After completing his Spitfire OTU in July 1941 he spent short periods with Nos 132, 485, 602 and 411 Sqns. On 3 June 1942 he flew a Spitfire to Malta, taking off from the aircraft carrier *Eagle*, and upon arrival on the island was assigned to No 603 Sqn, with whom he scored his first aerial victory on the 23rd – a Macchi C.202. In August McLeod was posted to No 1435 Sqn as a flight commander. In October his tour in Malta ended and he returned to Canada, where he spent several months as an instructor at the fighter OTU at Bagotville. Early in 1944 he returned to England, and in February was promoted to Squadron Leader and appointed commander of No 443 Sqn. McLeod led the unit throughout the period of the Normandy invasion, building up his victory score as the weeks passed by. On 27 September 1944 his unit was involved in a combat with several well flown Bf 109Gs over Holland, and he was shot down and killed. At the time of his death he was the second top-scoring Canadian pilot with 21 aircraft destroyed (of which 8 were achieved while flying Spitfire Mk IXs), 3 probably destroyed and 12 and 1 shared damaged.

WG CDR
WILLIAM VERNON CRAWFORD-COMPTON

Born in Invercargill, New Zealand, Crawford-Compton joined the RAF in 1939. He began his career as a fighter pilot early in 1941 when he joined No 603 Sqn with Spitfire Mk Vs, as a Sergeant. In May he received his commission and was posted to No 485 Sqn. Here he achieved his first victory on 13 October 1941 when he shot down a Bf 109F over France, and by the end of April 1942 Crawford-Compton's victory score stood at six aircraft destroyed and one shared, but then he broke his wrist in a crash landing and was taken off operations. The following August he joined No 611 Sqn, equipped with Spitfire Mk IXs, as a flight commander, before moving in December to take command of No 64 Sqn with Mk IXs. In June 1943, following promotion to Wing Commander, Crawfor-Compton was appointed leader of the Hornchurch Wing. In the following October he went to the USA to lecture on air fighting tactics, and upon his return to England was appointed leader of No 145 Wg, operating Spitfire Mk IXs. Early in 1945 Crawford-Compton moved to a staff appointment at No 11 Grp HQ, and remained there until the end of the conflict. His final score stood at 20 (possibly 21) enemy aircraft destroyed

(14 while flying Spitfire Mk IXs) and 1 shared destroyed, 3 and 1 shared probably destroyed and 13 damaged. After the war he continued in the RAF and attained the rank of Air Vice-Marshal.

FLT LT RAYMOND BROWN HESSELYN

Born in Invercargill, New Zealand, Hesselyn joined the RNZAF in 1940. In February 1942 he was posted to No 234 Sqn as a Sergeant, but shortly afterwards he was chosen to take part in the operation to fly the first batch of Spitfire Mk Vs to Malta. He made the flight on 9 March, flying from the aircraft carrier *Eagle*, and upon his arrival on Malta he was allocated to No 249 Sqn, with whom he was credited with 11 victories (and received his commission) during the next five months. Hesselyn returned to the UK in July 1942, and for the next year served mainly with second-line flying units. In July 1943 he was posted to No 222 Sqn, flying Spitfire Mk IXs, and continued to build up his score. In September he was promoted to Flight Lieutenant and appointed a Flight Commander. About a month later, on 3 October, Hesselyn was involved in a combat with Bf 109Gs over Northern France and was seen to shoot one down before he was himself shot out the sky – he bailed out with leg wounds and was taken prisoner. After his return from captivity Hesselyn claimed to have shot down three enemy aircraft during his final combat, but the last two were not officially confirmed. His victory score stood at 18 enemy aircraft destroyed, plus possibly 2 more (of which 6 or 8 were achieved while flying Spitfire Mk IXs), 1 shared destroyed, 2 probably destroyed and 7 damaged. After the war he stayed in the RAF and attained the rank of Squadron Leader.

GRP CAPT
WILFRED DUNCAN-SMITH

Born in Madras, India, Duncan-Smith joined the RAF in 1939. He began his career as a fighter pilot in October 1940 when he joined No 611 Sqn as a Sergeant flying Spitfire Mk Is. Early in 1941 he was commissioned and he opened his victory score on 18 June when, flying a Spitfire Mk V, he was credited with the destruction of a Bf 109E. In August he was posted to No 603 Sqn as a flight commander, but shortly afterwards was taken ill and he spent the rest of the year in hospital. After his recovery Duncan-Smith spent a few months with No 411 Sqn, before being promoted in April 1942 to Squadron Leader and taking command of No 64 Sqn – he was still incumbent when the unit became the first in Fighter Command to receive the Spitfire Mk IX. In August 1942 he was promoted to Wing Commander and led the North Weald Wing in action. Upon completion of the tour Duncan-Smith had a spell as staff officer at headquarters Fighter Command, then in May 1943 he was posted to Malta were he led the Luqa Wing for a short period, before being sent to North Africa to lead No 244 Wg of the Desert Air Force. Promoted to Group Captain in November 1943, he took command of No 324 Wg operating in the Mediterranean area, and held that post until March 1945. At the end of the war Duncan-Smith's victory score stood at 17 enemy aircraft destroyed and 2 shared, 6 and 2 shared probably destroyed and 8 damaged. All of his victories were scored while flying Spitfires, and more than half of them were achieved while flying the Mk IX. After the war he continued in the RAF as a Group Captain.

WG CDR RAYMOND HARRIES

Born in South Wales, Harries joined the RAF early in the war. After completing his training he gained his commission and spent a short time with No 43 Sqn, then went to No 58 OTU as an instructor. In February 1942 he was posted to No 131 Sqn, with Spitfire Mk Vs, as a Flight Commander. He opened his victory score on 12 March when he shared in the destruction of a Ju 88 over North Wales. Throughout the year he built up his score and in December he was promoted to Squadron Leader. Harries took command of No 91 Sqn, flying Spitfire Mk Vs until April 1943

Flg Off Irving 'Hap' Kennedy flew Spitfire Mk IXs with No 111 Sqn, from Sicily in September 1943. A Canadian, his eventual victory score was 10 enemy aircraft destroyed, 5 shared destroyed and 1 probably destroyed. Aside from 'Treble One', Kennedy saw action with Nos 249, 185, 93 and 401 Sqns, and flew exclusively Spitfires of varying marks – VC, VIII, IX and IXB

The Normandy invasion saw many of the RAF's leading aces adding to their scores in heavy fighting over the beachhead. Losses were felt on both sides, however, as this photo illustrates – Spitfire LF IX ZD-C of No 222 Sqn crashed on the French coast soon after D-Day after being hit by flak. Note the crudely painted invasion stripes and unit ID codes which were hastily added during the afternoon and evening of D-1. The degree of care with which these were applied varied from unit to unit

when the unit re-equipped with Spitfire Mk XIIs. In the following August he was promoted to Wing Commander and led the Westhampnett Wing, comprising the two Mk XII squadrons, until December. He then went to the USA to lecture on tactics, and in the spring of 1944 became leader of No 135 Wg with Spitfire Mk IXs. In January 1945 Harries returned to England to convert to the Tempest, in preparation for the re-equipment of the whole of the Wing with this type. However, before his command returned to action Harries was appointed to a staff post at No 84 Grp headquarters, and remained there until the end of the war. At the end of the conflict his victory score stood at 15 enemy aircraft destroyed and 3 shared, 2 probably destroyed and 5 and 1 shared damaged. All of his kills were achieved while flying Spitfires, and Harries was also the most successful pilot to fly the Mk XII in action, scoring 10 and 1 shared victory while flying this variant. After the war he continued in the RAF, but sadly was killed in a flying accident in 1950.

THE TACTICS OF THE ACES

By the summer of 1942, when the Spitfire Mk IX entered service, RAF fighter tactics were based on the pair of aircraft as the smallest fighting unit. When in battle formation the number two flew some 250 yards from the leader, almost abreast but both slightly behind and below. In this way each pilot had a clear view into the blind zone behind the other's aircraft, making it difficult for an enemy fighter to deliver an attack without being seen in good time. It was the number two's duty to stay with his leader at all times and cover his tail. Normally the number two did not fire his guns except in defence of the leader, or unless specifically ordered to do so – for example if the leader had set up a surprise attack on two or more enemy aircraft. Two such pairs of fighters worked together as a four, and three such fours worked together as a squadron.

The technique followed by most of the ace pilots to build up their scores was essentially simple, though it required considerable personal skill to make it work. The first requirement was to see the enemy first and, having done so, to be able to take in the tactical situation in that area of sky at a glance. Then, if possible without being seen by the enemy, they moved into a position usually above and up-sun of the prey. From there they would pounce on the enemy in high speed descent, announcing their presence with a series of short and usually accurate bursts of fire. After delivering the attack they usually zoomed back into position above the enemy aircraft, ready to deliver another strike should this be necessary.

Ace pilots were usually very good shots, however, and one such attack was usually sufficient to send an enemy plane tumbling from the sky shedding pieces.

As an example of this type of action let us take a look at Wg Cdr 'Johnnie' Johnson's 15th aerial victory, scored on 24 June 1943. He was leading his Wing as they provided top cover for Ramrod 164 – an attack by RAF Venturas on

An armourer of No 303 'Warsaw-Kosciuszko' Sqn loads the starboard Hispano 20 mm cannon with its complement of 120 rounds. The difference between a successful air combat and abject frustration on the pilot's behalf often boiled down to the careful loading of cannon shells and machine gun bullets. A gun jam during a high-g dogfight was, sadly, an all too common occurrence for RAF fighter pilots during World War 2 (Salkeld)

A Spitfire Mk IX of No 310 'Czech' Sqn is levelled off on a tail jack prior to the all-important harmonisation of the gunsight and guns taking place. A common occurrence on fighter stations across the UK during World War 2, this photograph was taken at Appledram, home for elements of the Tangmere Wing, in June 1944 (Hurt)

Yainville power-station in France. He later noted in his combat report:

'I was leading Kenley Wing on Ramrod 106 and was over the target area (Yainville) 17.25 hours. Operations warned me of E/A climbing up inland and I orbited the Wing, and shortly afterwards saw 40 E/A climbing up from Rouen towards Le Havre. Although not possessing tactical advantage these E/As were immediately engaged in order to keep them from molesting the bombers, but with no conclusive results. The Wing was reformed and after trying to engage three Fw 190s headed from Rouen area towards Fecamp. At this time two Fw 190s were seen shadowing the Wing and obviously waiting to bounce the odd straggler. They were about two miles behind the Wing and I climbed both squadrons steeply into sun and carried out one orbit to port. The Fw 190s who were then down sun of us appeared to loose sight of the Wing and flew beneath us presenting an excellent target. They were seen 1000 ft below my section, and one mile ahead I ordered my number two, Sqn Ldr McNair, to engage them with me, and the remainder of the Squadron were told to keep high in order not to scare the Huns. I closed on number two E/A from line astern and opening fire from 300 yds closed to 150 yds. Cannon strikes were seen on the fuselage and tailplane, and a large piece fell away from the starboard half of his tail unit. The E/A spun down and crashed at Valmont.'

Subsequent analysis of the combat film revealed that Johnson fired three bursts at the Fw 190 – one of 0.7 seconds from 360 yards, then one lasting 0.3 seconds, then the main burst lasting 4.9 seconds closing from 240 yards. The film revealed strikes on the port wing of the German fighter, before the dense cloud of black smoke issuing from the aircraft obscured it. Sqn Ldr Robert McNair quickly shot down the other Fw 190 of the pair.

Every fighter pilot sought to position himself to secure such a relatively easy victory, but to become an ace a pilot had also to have the determination to seek out and destroy enemy aircraft even when conditions were far from ideal. As an example of this, take a look at Sqn Ldr William Crawford-Compton's tenth victory on 20 January 1943. That afternoon he led No 64 Sqn with Spitfire Mk IXs in a sweep over the Straits of Dover.

'While leading No 64 Sqn we were informed by Ops of two to three enemy aircraft a ship off Calais. I dived down under a layer of cloud about 7000 ft and searched for the enemy aircraft for two or three minutes. I could not see them so called up to say we would attack the ship. I had started my dive when I saw seven Fw 190s about two miles away coming from Gris Nez. I pulled up sharply and managed to get above and behind without being seen. I fired a very short burst at the number four but they went into cloud and I saw no hits. I was attacked and broke away. One Fw 190 then closed in on my port and did not see me. I fired a second burst from slightly aside and below and saw hits on the fuselage and starboard wing root. I was using armour-piercing/incendiary (ammunition) which, when it hit, left a streak of flame about 18 inches long. The enemy aircraft began smoking furiously and headed for the coast. I fired another short burst and saw hits. It then caught fire and hit the water about 1000 yds off the shore half a mile east of Calais. I broke away and experienced heavy flak from the shore and the ship. About two minutes after this I saw another Fw 190 heading inland trailing grey smoke. We came back to mid-Channel at zero feet and then climbed to cloud height.'

Another qualification to be a fighter ace was the ability to handle an aircraft right to the limits of its manoeuvrability. As an example of this, observe the action during which Sqn Ldr 'Chris' Le Roux achieved his 17th victory. On 31 July 1944 he was leading No 602 Sqn on an armed reconnaissance over Normandy hunting for enemy vehicles.

'We had already attacked Met (mechanical transport) and were running short of ammo. Kenway (the ground controller) then asked us to investigate some Met in the Falaise area. I took my number two there and used up the rest of my ammo on the Met. I lost my number two and decided to make for home. Leaving the Falaise area at 3000 ft I was bounced by six Fw 190s at 9000 ft. I had no ammunition and had continuously to take violent evasive action. The E/A in turn tried to get on my tail. On each occasion I turned tightly to starboard and simulated attempts to get on his tail, since I did not want to let them know I was out of ammunition. On one occasion when we were at 300 ft I turned very tightly to starboard and got on an Fw 190's tail. He took violent evasive action, turning to starboard. Suddenly he stalled, flicked over on his back and crashed straight into the ground where he blew up. Being very short of fuel I landed at the first strip I saw which was A4 (landing ground at Deux Jumeaux). The enemy aircraft crashed about miles miles SW of Vire. I claim this Fw 190 destroyed.'

Even in combat there were rules of etiquette that junior ranking pilots were expected to observe, and not running out in front of the formation leader was one of them. On 10 September 1943 Flg Off Irving Kennedy, a Canadian serving with No 111 Sqn based at Falcone in Sicily, took part in a fighter sweep over Salerno in Italy where Allied troops were establishing positions ashore following the landings the previous day. Grp

Capt George Gilroy, commander of No 324 Wg, led the Spitfire Mk IXs in an attack on Fw 190 fighter-bombers attempting to bomb the troops coming ashore. The action developed into a tail chase which Kennedy described graphically in his autobiography *Black Crosses Off My Wingtip*. His mount was MA481, a brand new aircraft delivered to the unit a few days earlier, for what was to be his fifth victory:

'I trimmed the Spitfire to fly hands off, and started working my way through the pack of Spitfires from the back. It was like a horse race . . . I went by one after another, just weaving gently through the pack, barely above the trees, until I caught up with the leading Spitfire. This turned out to be the Group Captain who, as was the custom, had his own initials on the aircraft. Out in front of Grp Capt Gilroy, well out of range at about 800 yards, was the last Fw 190, smoking a little black at full throttle.

'I pulled up abreast of our Commander, just off his starboard wingtip. He looked over to his right at me, his face covered with his oxygen mask and mike. "Do I stay here or do I dare pass him?" I wondered. I pulled back just a touch on the throttle for a couple of minutes. We were not gaining an inch on the Focke-Wulf. It was a delightful situation because I knew that the Group Captain was primarily interested in the Wing. But it demanded tact. He was the Officer Commanding, but surely he wanted someone to get that Hun up ahead! So I tapped the throttle forward the last half inch, moved ahead (I must admit to a faint smile behind my oxygen mask), caught up to the Focke-Wulf pretty smartly, and hit him with a good clout with everything I had – that is with both cannons and machine guns. The German was a smart pilot. He pulled back on the stick at once, and shot straight up to 1500 ft, baled out very quickly, and was coming down on his parachute when the Group Captain went by him. "Who shot down that aircraft?" No call sign, but there was no mistaking the Group Captain's voice. Only five words, somewhat sharply, I still recall. "Blue Three here, sir", I answered, not quite sure what was coming. "Bloody good show! Let's go home chaps."'

SPITFIRE VERSUS V1 FLYING BOMB

During the early morning darkness on 13 June 1944 the Luftwaffe unleashed a new form of attack on London – the V1 flying bomb. Between then and the end of the month 2442 flying bombs were launched at the capital. Roughly one-third of the weapons, about 800 missiles, exploded on the Greater London built-up area where they caused 2441 deaths and 7107 cases of serious injury. The remainder, about two-thirds of the total, either crashed or were shot down by fighters or guns before reaching the target area.

It did not take the defenders long to gauge the nature of Luftwaffe's new retaliation weapon. The V1s were not manufactured to normal aircraft tolerances so there were large variations in performance. The majority flew at speeds around 350 mph, though the fastest were tracked at 420 mph and the slowest came in at around 230 mph. There were similar variations in altitude; most crossed the coast at between 3000 and 4000 ft, but the highest came in at 8000 ft and the lowest were at tree-top height (which usually lead to their early demise). The flight time from the launching sites to London was between 20 and 25 minutes.

Flt Lt G Armstrong, an Australian flying with No 165 Sqn, landed this 'toasted' Spitfire Mk IXB at Lympne on 1 July 1944, having flown through a cloud of burning fuel after his rounds detonated the warhead of a V1 *(IWM)*

SPITFIRE VERSUS V1 FLYING BOMB

In its final form the system to protect the capital from the V1s comprised four belts of defences. The first belt, running from mid-Channel to about ten miles short of the coast, was the Outer Fighter Patrol Area where Tempests, Mustangs and Spitfires and at night Mosquitoes engaged the flying bombs. Next came the Gun Belt, some 800 heavy AA guns and 1800 lighter weapons positioned along the coast between Beachy Head and Dover – fighters were forbidden to enter this zone, allowing the gunners freedom to shoot at anything that came within range. From the ten miles inland to ten miles short of London was the inner Fighter Patrol Area, where more fighters engaged the V1s. The fourth belt began ten miles short of the Greater London conurbation and ended at its outskirts; over this area about 1000 barrage balloons trailed cables to ensnare the missiles.

Initially the Spitfires engaging the V1s belonged to No 150 Wg based at Lympne, comprising Nos 1 and 165 Sqns with Mk IXs and No 41 Sqn with Mk XIIs. Neither version was fast enough at low altitude to engage the faster V1s, so the three units equipped with the Mk XIV (Nos 91, 322 and 610 Sqns) moved to airfields in Kent to assist in the defence of the capital. For these operations some Spitfire Mk XIVs had their engines modified to run on 150 octane petrol, allowing a maximum of +25 lbs boost to be used; this increased the fighter's speed by about 30 mph at low altitude, to about 400 mph at 2000 ft.

Of the V1s destroyed by fighter cannon fire, about 90 per cent went down out of control and detonated when they hit the ground. The remaining ten per cent detonated in mid-air, but provided the fighter was more than 150 yards away from the explosion there was little risk of serious damage. Minor damage was sometimes caused by flying through a cloud of burning petrol from the missile's fuel tank, or by striking pieces of metal hurled in all directions by the force of the explosion.

Firing at the missiles from short range could be a hazardous business, however. On 3 August Capt Jean Marie Maridor, a French pilot flying Spitfire Mk XIVs with No 91 Sqn, was pursuing a flying bomb heading towards the military hospital at Benenden. He closed to short range to ensure the destruction of the missile and opened fire, but the warhead detonated wrecking the fighter and killing its brave pilot – Maridor was credited with the destruction of 11 flying bombs.

In flight the V1 was controlled by its elevators and rudder; it had no ailerons, and that made it vulnerable to any interference in the rolling plane. One method fighter pilots used was to fly alongside the missile, place a wing tip under that of the flying bomb and then bank steeply to flip the missile out of control. On 20 August Flt Sgt Paul Leva, a Belgian with No 350 Sqn based at Hawkinge, was operating in the inner Fighter Patrol Area. Flying one of his unit's recently acquired Spitfire Mk XIVs, he employed this technique to bring down a V1. Later he wrote:

'. . . the bomb went unscathed through the two first defence lines and, directed by the controller, I duly spotted the ugly little brute with the glowing tail below me. I banked to enter a steep dive, gathering speed and getting nearer and nearer to my target.

'Alas, though, I was not near enough. Soon, with my speed dropping after levelling off, I could see that the distance separating us did not diminish any more and even began to increase.

'Utterly disappointed, I nevertheless opened fire, aiming high to compensate for the distance. I had the happy surprise to see some impacts and bits flying off the wings.

'I fired burst after burst, damaging the bomb still more. Although no vital part was hit, its speed diminished and it entered a shallow dive.

'My hopes went soaring again, I was now approaching my target so fast that I had to throttle back. Ready for the kill, I positioned myself at what I estimated was the right distance. I depressed the trigger, but instead of the staccato of firing bullets I heard only the whistling sound of escaping compressed air.

'The voice of the controller came on again: "Any luck?"

'"No", I said forlornly. "I damaged it, but have no ammunition left. Its very slow now and losing height. I am practically flying in formation with it."

'"Tough luck", said the controller. "Time to turn back now - you are getting very near the balloon barrage."

'It was then that suddenly, spurred no doubt by my frustration, I remembered the briefing of the intelligence officer, who earlier had spoken of sending V1s out of control by tipping up one wing.

A Spitfire Mk IX pilot formates on a V1, preparatory to sending the latter down out of control. This could be done by knocking up the wing of the flying bomb, which invariably resulted in some damage to the wing of the fighter itself, or by placing the Spitfire's wing over that of the flying bomb to destroy the lift on that side *(IWM)*

'"Wait," I said. "I think I can try something." Adjusting the throttle I eased myself forward until I came abreast the bomb. What a sight it was at close range! The wings were so ragged with the impact of the bullets that I wondered how it could still fly almost straight and level.

'Positioning myself slightly underneath, I placed my starboard wing tip under the port wing of the bomb. I came up slowly, made contact with it as softly as I could, and then moved the stick violently back and to the left.

'This made me enter a steep climbing turn and I lost sight of the bomb. I continued turning fast through 360 degrees, then I saw it well below me, going down steeply, hitting the ground and exploding with a blinding flash.'

When Leva landed at Hawkinge it was found that the fighter's wing tip was badly bent where it had been in contact with the V1, and it had to be replaced.

There was a more elegant method to dispose of a V1, if a fighter could move into a position alongside it. The pilot edged his wing *over the top* of that of the V1, thus destroying the lift on one side of the flying bomb. That sent the V1 into a steep bank and out of control, but without the need for physical contact between the two aircraft so there was no damage to the fighter.

Such tactics were of value only against V1s that were flying relatively slowly – the great majority of V1s destroyed by fighters fell to cannon and machine gun fire. Three days after Leva knocked the V1 out of control, Flt Lt T Spencer of No 41 Sqn achieved the rare feat of destroying two missiles in a single sortie. The fact that he was flying the Spitfire Mk XII, which was slower than the Mk XIV, combined with the poor weather conditions to make his accomplishment all the more remarkable. The report on the action stated:

'Red Section (two aircraft) airborne 0805 to 0915 from Lympne, under Kingsley 11 Control on Ashford (area) Patrol, was informed that a flying bomb was approaching East of Folkestone. Seeing AA fire Flt Lt T Spencer dived from 9000 ft to 2000 ft and saw Diver (code-name for V1) at 10 o'clock 1000ft above, over a point some two miles south of Mersham in hazy visibility. The Diver at 3000ft on course 310 degrees was travelling at 240 mph.

Climbing, Flt Lt Spencer opened fire with one and two second bursts. Closing from 250 yards to 80 yards from astern and slightly below, seeing strikes on the jet. He overshot the Diver and saw it go down near railway line at approximately R 5056 at 0820 hours.

On the same patrol and under Kingsley 11 Control from Ashford Flt Lt Spencer was informed that Diver would pass four miles due west of Ashford. Seeing flares (fired from Observer Corps posts on the ground to indicate the passage of a V1 overhead), he dived from 10,000 ft and saw the Diver at two o'clock. Closed and saw no strikes from four-second burst. A second burst of two seconds obtained strikes on port side of the fuselage and port wing root. The petrol tank exploded with black smoke and the Diver flicked to port and went in north of railway line near Harrietsham R 3171 at 0907 hours. Diver was at 2500ft on 340 degrees doing 360 mph. Weather hazy.'

Spencer shot down a total of six flying bombs, all while flying the Spitfire Mk XII.

The Spitfire pilots that scored best against the V1s all flew Mk XIVs. Dutchman Flg Off R Burgwal of No 322 Sqn was credited with 21 missiles destroyed, whilst Sqn Ldr N Kynaston and Flt Lt R Nash, both of No 91 Sqn, were credited with 17 and 16$^{1}/_{2}$ flying bombs respectively.

At the end of August 1944, Allied ground forces advancing along the north coast of France overran the last of the V1 launching sites in the Pas de Calais. The 8617th and last flying bomb launched from that area crossed the south coast of England on the morning of 1 September.

FOUR MAJOR IMPROVEMENTS

Throughout the war the Spitfire was subjected to many hundreds of modifications aimed at improving its performance and fighting capabilities, or reducing its failings. In the summer and autumn of 1944 four major improvements incorporated in Spitfire fighter variants at that time deserve special mention in this account. In order of their entry into service they were: the installation of the gyro gunsight, the fitting of the 'E' Type wing and armament, the fitting of the bubble canopy, together with a redesigned and cut-back rear fuselage, and the installation of additional fuel tanks in the rear fuselage. These modifications greatly increased the fighting ability of the Spitfire, though neither singly nor collectively were they considered sufficiently important to warrant the issue of a new mark number. The modifications, described in more detail below, were applied to the three Spitfire variants then in large scale production – the Mks IX, XIV and XVI.

THE GYRO GUNSIGHT

In action the effectiveness of a fighter's cannon and machine guns depends on the pilot's ability to aim the rounds with sufficient accuracy to score hits on the target. During the mid-war period RAF fighters carried the simple GM2 reflector gunsight. This provided an illuminated fixed aiming point in the centre of the reflector glass, surrounded by a fixed circle which helped the pilot judge the correct deflection angle when engaging a manoeuvring or crossing target. In fact the ability to judge the deflection angle accurately in the heat of the battle was one of the main points that separated the ace pilots from the also-rans.

Early in the war it was realised that if an automatic device could be developed to indicate to the pilot the correct amount of deflection to use when firing during a turning combat, this would greatly enhance

The gyro gunsight, as fitted in the cockpit of this Spitfire Mk IX, proved a revelation for many young fighter pilots who lacked the ability to perform accurate deflection shooting like the high-scoring aces of Fighter Command. Having struggled for years to judge lead distances with the rudimentary GM2 reflector sight, average shots now found that effective 'systems management' when it came to aligning the sighting graticule was virtually all that was needed to obtain accuracy with even the greatest angles of deflection *(Murland)*

the effectiveness of the fighter force. Following four years of hard work at the Royal Aircraft Establishment at Farnborough, the Mk II Gyro Gunsight went into large scale production at the end of 1943.

This device worked on the principal that if a fighter pilot followed an enemy aircraft in the turn and held his gunsight on the latter, his rate of turn was proportional to the deflection angle required to hit the enemy. A gyroscope measured his rate of turn, and tilted a mirror which moved the position of the sighting graticule to show the required deflection angle. The required deflection varied with range, however, so the gunsight incorporated a simple system of optical rangefinding. Before the engagement the pilot set on the sight the approximate wingspan of the enemy aircraft. As he closed on his foe, the pilot operated a control mounted on the throttle arm which altered the diameter of the sighting graticule so that it size matched the wingspan of the enemy aircraft. Since the wingspan of the target aircraft had been set on the sight, the adjustment of the graticule 'told' the gunsight the range of the target. An analogue computer in the gunsight worked out the correct point ahead of the target at which the pilot should aim in order to score hits.

Once fighter pilots got used to the new sight and learned its foibles, the general accuracy of deflection shooting improved dramatically. During 1944 an analysis of 130 combats by Spitfire Mk IXs fitted with fixed-graticule sights revealed that there had been 34 kills – 26 per cent of the total. During the same period, one squadron operating the same Spitfire variant fitted with the new gunsight took part in 38 combats, scoring 19 kills – 50 per cent of the total. The new gunsight virtually doubled the effectiveness of air-to-air gunnery. With the new sight, pilots reported scoring hits on evading targets at ranges as great as 600 yards, and at deflection angles of up to 50 degrees.

Many aces refused to have the new gunsight in their aircraft, however. It was larger than its predecessor, and it restricted visibility in the all-important sector in front of the aircraft. Moreover, the pilot had track the target for few seconds to allow the computer to work out the correct deflection angle. There were a few exceptionally gifted pilots who could judge the correct deflection angle at a glance, and for them the disadvantages of the gyro gunsight outweighed its advantages.

Yet, by definition, exceptional pilots were few and far between, and they could not win an air war by themselves. The combat the capability of a fighter force depended on the shooting ability of the *average* squadron pilot, rather than that of the few aces. It is difficult to exaggerate the value of the gyro gunsight in assisting the Allied air forces to maintain air superiority during the final year of the war, when their piston-engined fighters had to battle with the much-faster German jet types. The improvement in air-to-air gunnery brought about by the new gunsight helped to compensate for the huge difference in performance. As a result Allied fighters shot down an average of more than two German jet fighters for each Allied fighter or bomber destroyed by the jets.

The value of the new sight when engaging jets is evident from the combat report of Flt Lt 'Tex' Davenport of No 401 Sqn, when he and other members of the Canadian unit shared in the destruction of the first Me 262 to fall to the Spitfire, on 5 October 1944 – note the ranges and the deflection angles at which he was able to score hits:

The gyro gunsight in action, showing the sighting picture. Having selected the wingspan of the target aircraft by rotating the switch on the front of the sight, the pilot then manipulated a control mounted on the throttle arm to vary the diameter of the circle so that it matched the size of the wingspan of the enemy aircraft. He then held the target in the centre of the circle for a few seconds to give the device time to calculate the deflection angle necessary to achieve hits. During the final year of the war the new gunsight greatly increased the effectiveness of Allied air gunnery

Flg Off Hugh Murland of No 74 Sqn pictured with a Mk XVIE Spitfire fitted with a bubble canopy. This new device gave greatly improved visibility to the rear and below, making it easier to see an enemy fighter before it could reach a position to deliver a surprise attack. Ironically, despite calls for improved rear-hemisphere visiblity from Fighter Command pilots as early as 1939, the cut down rear deck and 'bubble' canopy only appeared for the final months of the war when the threat posed by the Luftwaffe was at its lowest in six years of bitter conflict *(Murland)*

`I was flying as Yellow 1, No 401 "Blackout" Sqn when we sighted an Me 262 at 12,000 ft, five miles north-east of Nijmegen. There was a great mix-up as all 12 Spits dove for the jet job. I waited until he made his first break then came in 20 degs line astern at approx 450 miles an hour. I gave a three-second burst at 400 yards and observed strikes on the fuselage. I then continued the chase which was composed of rolls, dives and turns at approx 375 mph. I finally closed into 300 yards line astern and emptied the remainder of my guns, approximately 10 or 12 seconds, into the kite, observing strikes all in engines and fuselage. The A/C was burning all this time. The pilot seemed to be unhurt and put up a good fight all during this, at the last realising the fight was up he attempted to ram Red 1 on the way to the ground, when he crashed and burned. I used camera and got eight feet of film, cannon, MG. Gyro sight functioned properly. No ammunition left. I claim 1/5 Me 262 destroyed.'

THE 'E' TYPE WING AND ARMAMENT

Until the summer of 1944 fighter variants of the Spitfire were built with the `C' Type wing, and the standard armament was two 20 mm Hispano cannon each with 120 rounds of ammunition, and four .303-in machine guns each with 350 rounds.

During a turning combat the value of the four Browning .303-in guns mounted in the outer wing was questionable. If the pilot was pulling `G' when he fired, the flexing of the fighter's wings ensured that rounds set out in a quite different direction from where the gunsight was pointing. Another factor mitigating against the value of .303-in weapons at this stage of the war was that virtually all combat aircraft carried armour protection, which rifle-calibre rounds could not penetrate.

By 1944 the US factories were producing the Browning .5-in machine gun in such large numbers that the weapon was made available in quantity to the RAF. The Spitfire wing was redesigned to take the weapon, and the so-called 'E' Type had the cannon and machine guns re-positioned. The 20 mm cannon was moved from the inboard cannon positions to the outboard positions, about a foot further out. A .5-in machine gun, and a box with 250 rounds of ammunition, was installed in the space vacated by the cannon and its magazine. The .5-in weapons delivered a heavier penetrative punch than the smaller guns they replaced, and were far more effective for both air-to-air and air-to-ground firing.

THE BUBBLE CANOPY

In the majority of cases where an aircraft was shot down in fighter-versus-fighter combat, the victim never saw his assailant before it was too late to take effective evasive action. Most such attacks were mounted from the fighter's blind zone, below and behind, and many a pilot gained ace status by exploiting this weakness. Obviously, therefore, if the Spitfire could be modified to reduce the chances of a successful surprise attack by the enemy, its probability of survival in action would be correspondingly enhanced.

The answer was to cut back the rear fuselage behind the cockpit, and fit the fighter with a bubble canopy. A Spitfire Mk VIII modified in this way flew for the first time in mid-1943. The manufacturer's trials showed

This view of a Spitfire Mk XVIE of No 17 Sqn refuelling at Chivenor after the war clearly shows the size of the 'bubble' canopy, as well the degree of cutback built into the rear fuselage by Vickers-Armstrong

the change brought no significant deterioration in the aircaft's handling characteristics, and it went to the Air Fighting Development Unit at Duxford to allow experienced service pilots to fly it. The latter were hugely impressed with the increase in view to the rear and below brought about by the bubble canopy, and their report noted:

'This is an enormous improvement over the standard Spitfire rear view. The pilot can see quite easily round to his fin and past it, almost to the further edge of the tailplane; ie, if he looks over his left shoulder he can practically see to the starboard tip of the tail. By banking the aircraft slightly during weaving action, the downward view to the rear is opened up well.'

Production Spitfire Mk IXs, XIVs and XVIs fitted with bubble canopies began reaching operational squadrons early in 1945, and they immediately became popular with pilots.

ADDITIONAL FUEL TANKS IN THE REAR FUSELAGE

From the time the Spitfire began to take part in offensive air operations over enemy territory, its short radius of action was a source of embarrassment to those who flew the aircraft. The installation of a drop tank under the fuselage was one answer, but the tanks caused additional drag, and moreover they had to be jettisoned before the aircraft went into action. The Mks VIII and XIV, and late-production versions of the Mk XII, had small additional tanks fitted in the wing leading edge, close to the fuselage. But the extra fuel thus carried, between $25^1/2$ and 28 gallons, did little more than compensate for the higher rates of consumption of the fighters' more powerful Merlin or Griffon engines.

The best way to increase the Spitfire's radius of action was to install a couple of larger tanks in the rear fuselage. In the case of late production Mk IXs and XVIs, these tanks had a total capacity of 72 Imp gallons (64 gallons in aircraft fitted with a bubble canopy). Late production Mk XIVs had rear fuselage tanks with a total capacity of 75 gallons (64 gallons in

73

French Canadian Flt Lt Dick Audet was serving with No 411 'Grizzly Bear' Sqn when he opened his 'account' in spectacular fashion on 29 December 1944 by downing five aircraft in quick succession. In the month that followed he gained several other victories before being killed on 3 March 1945 when his aircraft was hit by flak during a strafing mission. At the time of his death Audet's score stood at 10 aircraft destroyed and 1 shared destroyed, 1 aircraft damaged and 1 destroyed on the ground

Spitfire Mk IXs of No 411 Sqn warm their engines before a mission from B88/Heesch in Holland in December 1944. Each aircraft carries a 30 gallon slipper tank, the configuration of Dick Audet's aircraft when he took off for his famous sortie on the 29th of that month. Silhouetted against the windscreen of the Spitfire nearest to the camera is the head of the gyro gunsight *(Public Archives of Canada)*

aircraft fitted with a bubble canopy, only one tank with 31 gallons in the fighter reconnaissance version). The additional fuel gave the Spitfire a greatly increased operational radius of action during the final months of the war.

THE REMARKABLE FEAT OF DICK AUDET

No description of late mark Spitfire aces is complete without mention of the short but brilliant career of the French Canadian Richard 'Dick' Audet. Audet gained his wings in October 1942 and was sent to England, but once there he spent most of the next two years flying with second line units, including an army co-operation squadron engaged in towing banner targets for AA gunners. These humdrum tasks allowed him to build up a large number of flying hours, however, and amass considerable experience in aircraft handling. In September 1944, with the rank of Flt Lt, he was posted to No 411 Sqn equipped with Spitfire Mk IXs, and the following month he was appointed flight commander. By 28 December 1944 he had flown 52 operational sorties, but although he had made several attacks on ground targets, he was never in the right place at the right time to engage enemy aircraft in the air.

That changed abruptly on 29 December. The 'Battle of the Bulge' was in full swing and the German fighter force was mounting a major effort to cover the take-off of Me 262 jet fighter-bombers from Rheine airfield near Osnabrück, to allow the latter to attack Allied troop positions in the Ardennes area. Soon after midday No 411 Sqn's Mk IXEs were scrambled from Heesch in Holland and directed to patrol over Rheine at 10,500 ft. Suddenly Audet, leading Yellow Section, caught sight of a dozen enemy fighters below.

'The enemy were four Messerschmitt 109s and eight Focke-Wulf 190s, flying line astern. I attacked an Me 109, the last aircraft in the formation. At 200 yds I opened fire and saw strikes all over the fuselage and wing roots. The '109 quickly burst into flames and was seen to trail black smoke.

'I now went around in a defensive circle until I spotted an Fw 190. I attacked from 250 yards down to 100 yards and from 30 degrees from line astern. I saw strikes over the cockpit and to the rear of the fuselage. It burst into flames. I saw the pilot slumped in his cockpit.

'Ahead was a 109 going down in a slight dive. It pulled up sharply into

Two Mk IXs from No 317 'City of Wilno' Sqn are bombed up and plugged in to their respective acc trolleys in preparation for a short-notice scramble from Grimbergen in January 1945 (via Jerry Scutts)

A Spitfire Mk IX fighter-bomber of No 132 Sqn receives its load of two 250-lb bombs and one 500-lb device. The bombs all have nose pistols so as to detonate the weapons with the minimum possible delay after striking the ground (via Bruce Robertson)

a climb, and the cockpit canopy flew off. I gave a short burst at about 300 yds and the aircraft whipped down in a dive. The pilot attempted to bail out, but his chute ripped to shreds. I saw the 109 hit the ground and smash into flaming pieces.

'I next spotted an Fw 190 being pursued by a Spitfire pursued in turn by an Fw 190. I called this pilot – one of my Yellow Section – to break, and attacked the '109 from the rear. We went down in a steep dive. I opened fire at 250 yards and it burst into flames. I saw it go into the ground and burn.

'Several minutes later, while attempting to re-form my section, I spotted an Fw 190 at about 2000 ft. I dived on him and he turned into me from the right. He then flipped around in a left-hand turn, and attempted

a head-on attack. I slowed down to wait for him to fly into range. At about 200 yards I gave a short burst. I could not see any strikes but he flicked violently and continued to do so until he crashed.'

Audet made good use of his gyro gunsight during the action and his achievement – five enemy fighters shot down in the course of a single sortie – was witnessed by other pilots in his squadron, and confirmed independently by analysis of his combat camera film.

During the same action other pilots in his unit claimed the destruction of three enemy fighters. The three German units involved in the covering operation, *Jagdgeschwader* 6, 27 and 54, all suffered very heavy losses that day; evidence suggests that the three Fw 190s claimed by Audet all belonged to the 9th Staffel of JG 54.

Dick Audet received the DFC for his feat and, having gained ace status in a single sortie, went on to demonstrate that it had been no fluke. In the course of January 1945 he added five more aerial victories to his score, including an Me 262. On 3 March Audet was killed when his aircraft was shot down by flak during a strafing attack on a railway siding. At the time of his death, Audet's victory score stood at ten enemy aircraft destroyed and one shared destroyed, one aircraft damaged and one destroyed on the ground.

Sqn Ldr Witold Rettinger, commander of No 308 'City of Krakow' Sqn, is pictured with his Mk IX in the autumn of 1944 at Ghent, in Belgium. At that time the unit was engaged predominantly in fighter-bomber operations, and the aircraft carries 31 bombing mission symbols on the nose as well as sobriquet *Lala*, the nickname of his girlfriend. Flying Spitfire Mk IIAs and Vs with the same unit in 1941, Rettinger was credited with the destruction of four aircraft destroyed and two damaged *(Dr Koniarek Archives)*

Above left and left Spitfire Mk IXE of No 74 Sqn fitted with two 60-lb rockets and one 500-lb bomb. The rockets were not popular with the unit's pilots, who considered them a poor substitute for a pair of 250-lb bombs as was usually carried under the wings. These photographs show well the revised armament layout that came with the 'E' Type wing, the 20 mm Hispano cannon being mounted in the outboard position with the .5-in Browning machine gun immediately inboard *(Murland)*

Above Spitfire HF IX of *Groupe de Chasse* 2/7 `Nice' (previously No 326 Sqn) a French Air Force unit with the 1er *Corps Aerienne Français*, subordinated to the US 1st Tactical Air Force, is seen taxying out in the snow and slush at Luxeuil during the bitter winter of 1944-45. This unit was just one of a clutch of Free French squadrons that were formed in late 1943 in preparation for the coming invasion of Europe. Like the others, GC 2/7 was exclusively equipped with various models of Spitfire throughout its brief career *(via Bruce Robertson)*

Above right Unlike GC 2/7, the owners of this Spitfire Mk IX had been a part of the RAF since November 1941. No 340 'Ile de France' Sqn flew a succession of different versions of Spitfire from the Mk IIA through to the LF XVI. By the time this photograph was taken in the UK in late 1944, the unit's designation had changed to GC 4/2, and the French tri-colour and full rudder stripes had replaced the RAF roundel and fin flash. It also wears the familiar 'Cross of Lorraine' just under the canopy, a symbol adopted by No 340 Sqn several years previously *(via Jerry Scutts)*

By May 1945 a total of 964 Spitfire Mk IXs had been delivered to the Soviet Air Force, and this version duly saw service with several frontline units. These aircraft belonged to the 26th Guards Fighter Regiment, based in the Leningrad area, and differed from their RAF counterparts in being equipped with HF radios rather than VHF sets, as the Soviet Air Force did not use the latter *(via Geust)*

The close of World War 2 marked an end to the Spitfire's glory days, though in the years that followed the fighter continued to serve with a score of air forces around the world. It saw action in half a dozen small scale conflicts, though in only one of them – the Arab-Israeli conflict in 1948 and 1949 – did it engage in air-to-air combat. The last frontline RAF fighter squadron to operate Spitfires, No 80 with Mk 24s based in Hong Kong, finally gave them up early in 1952. The last to use the Spitfire in action was the Burmese Air Force, which operated the type in the ground attack role against rebel forces almost to the end of the 1950s.

When the Spitfire passed out of service in Burma the operational life of Reginald Mitchell's little fighter finally came to an end. It spanned the period from 1938 to 1958, the two most turbulent decades of the 20th Century which, in aviation terms, marked the transition from the era of the biplane to that of the Mach 2 fighter.

AUSTRALIAN SPITFIRE ACES 1942-45 BY STEWART WILSON

Australian pilots had a long association with the Spitfire during World War 2, flying Reginald Mitchell's famous fighter both with the Royal Australian Air Force (RAAF) 'at home' against the Japanese, and with the RAF in Europe and the Middle East against the Axis powers and in the Far East against Japan.

The outbreak of war in September 1939 saw all three Australian services rally to the cause with many thousands of servicemen heading to the northern hemisphere to assist Britain in her fight against Nazi Germany. Many Australian airmen joined the RAF direct, while others who graduated from the Empire Air Training Scheme formed the basis of the RAAF squadrons which operated in Europe under the control of the RAF flying their aircraft. Four of these squadrons – Nos 451, 453, 452 and 457 – operated Spitfires at some time during their histories, the latter pair flying the aircraft exclusively.

A total of 656 Spitfires was delivered to the RAAF between August 1942 and June 1945, and the serial prefix A58 was allocated to them. The first 246 were Mk Vs comprising 245 F VCs (A58-1 to 162, 164 to 185 and 200 to 259) plus a single F VB (A58-163). Included in the Mk V total is one example delivered in 1943 which was never given an RAAF serial, instead keeping the British serial EE731. Of interest is the fact that A58-259, delivered in November 1943, was the last Spitfire Mk V to be built at the Castle Bromwich factory.

Deliveries of the faster and more capable Spitfire Mk VIII began in October 1943, the 410 of this mark obtained comprising a mixture of F, LF and HF VIII variants. The Mk VIIIs were serialled A58-300 to 550 and A58-600 to 758. Many of the later Spitfire Mk VIIIs were delivered directly to storage and never flown operationally.

There were some problems with the Spitfire's early Australian service, mainly due to its short range and a lack of proper tactics. An incident in May 1943

Showing off his newly received 'stripes' to signify his promotion to the dizzy heights of Flying Offcer, a battle-seasoned Larry Cronin poses in front of 'his' Spitfire Mk VIII at Tulihal in early March 1944. Painted on the unit's traditional ace of spades emblem, which was applied to all squadron aircraft, are Cronin's three German kills and solitary Japanese victory. Within a week of this snapshot being taken Cronin had bagged an 'Oscar' and damaged two others to become an ace *(via Neil Mackenzie)*

This Spitfire Mk VIII was flown by Sqn Ldr Eric Gibbs, OC of No 54 Sqn based at Darwin in April 1944. Unusually, the aircraft was fitted with both pointed wing tips and four 20 mm cannon. This rare combination was probably intended for operations against the high-flying Ki 46 'Dinah' reconnaissance aircraft which were about the only Japanese machine seen by No 1 Wg in the Northern Territory by this stage of the war. An ex-Coastal Command pilot, Gibbs was given charge of No 54 Sqn in April 1942, and led the unit out to Australia the following month. He ended the war credited with five enemy aircraft destroyed, one shared destroyed and five damaged, although all of these were achieved while flying Spitfire Mk Vs from Darwin in 1943

brought the issue to a head and forced a rethink of RAAF Spitfire operations. It started when 18 Japanese bombers escorted by 24 fighters were detected approaching Darwin. No 1 Wg scrambled to intercept, but despite the early warning, did not reach the enemy formation until after Darwin had been bombed. The battle which followed was fought at some distance from the Spitfires' base, and as a result their meagre fuel reserves were exhausted and five Spitfires ran out of fuel on the way back to base and were lost. From then on the fighters did not indulge in fuel gobbling dogfights but 'bounced' enemy formations in a hit and run manner. The situation improved from there.

Several other RAAF squadrons flew Spitfires including Nos 79 and 85, and all eventually re-equipped with Mk VIIIs. Nos 79, 452 and 457 were used in the 'island hopping' operations to the north of Australia as Japan was gradually forced back as the war progressed. Once they had reached the island of Morotai in the Halmaheras group in January 1945 they were united under the banner of No 80 (Fighter) Wg. Two RAF Spitfire squadrons – Nos 548 and 549 – remained in the Darwin area while the others pushed north.

By now the Spitfire squadrons in Australia had also been re-equipped with the greatly superior Mk VIIIs, but the aircraft and pilots of No 80 Wg were about to enter into a very frustrating period of service in what would pan out as the final months of the Pacific war. Little serious action was forthcoming, not only for the Spitfire pilots but also for the other RAAF units which were operating in the area as part of the recently established 1st Tactical Air Force.

Their duties mainly comprised 'mopping up' operations, consistently attacking the many still strong – but largely forgotten by their rapidly withdrawing comrades – pockets of Japanese resistance on the islands around Morotai and parts of New Guinea. These operations were carried out on the orders of the Supreme Commander, South West Pacific Area (Gen Douglas MacArthur) and meant that not only

One of the last RAF wartime Spitfire units to form was No 548 Sqn, who were activated along with No 549 Sqn at Lawntown, in Queensland, in December 1943 as replacement units for Nos 452 and 457 Sqns. The latter had received their marching orders to follow the war across the Pacific, thus potentially leaving No 1 Wg comprising of just No 54 Sqn. Both units received their first Spitfire LF VIIIs in April 1944, and deployed to Darwin after work-ups in June. Sadly for the pilots allocated to these units, the enemy had long since stopped raiding Australia, and neither squadron ever got to fire their guns in anger. This is a No 548 Sqn machine

No 548 Sqn up in strength for the cameras in mid-1944. Both units disbanded in Melbourne in October 1945 *(Glaser)*

was the Australian effort generally falling behind the American push to the Philippines, but the losses being sustained, both at the hands of the enemy and through inevitable operational accidents, were not considered worthwhile when balanced against the dubious gains made.

The reason for all this was MacArthur's almost obsessive desire to 'return to the Philippines', and thus fulfil the promise he'd made on leaving three years earlier. His triumphant return was to be seen as his and his alone, and he did not want Australians, or any other non Americans, to share in the glory.

The situation was regarded as intolerable by the Australian pilots who saw it as a waste of effort and lives. After all, here were RAAF units with many experienced and battle hardened pilots in their midst, with very little of significance to do. For a fighter pilot this was a poor substitute for aerial combat, and there was some dissent among senior RAAF pilots, including Australia's top scoring ace Grp Capt Clive

Caldwell, who commanded No 80 Wg's Spitfires. He was supported by Grp Capt Wilf Arthur, another ace, and the CO of No 81 Wg's Kittyhawks.

At the same time, there was a minor scandal brewing over alleged illegal trading of liquor in the islands with some senior RAAF officers involved. This, and the simmering operational problem were soon to be combined in one of the most notorious incidents in RAAF history, – the the so-called 'mutiny', or attempted resignation of eight senior officers including Caldwell and Arthur as a protest against the situation on Morotai.

The 'resignations' were of course only symbolic as an officer could not resign in wartime, but an enquiry was nevertheless established to investigate the pilots' grievances. They were found to have some basis and the RAAF hierarchy was sympathetic – these were war heroes with high national profiles after all – but the unprecendented action taken by them had to be seen to be punished in some way. This is where the liquor trading allegations came into play with the result that Grp Capt Caldwell and Sqn Ldr Bobby Gibbes (himself a double ace) were court martialled for using RAAF transport aircraft for illegal liquor trafficking with the Americans! Both were reduced in rank.

The end of the war with Japan saw the Spitfire's RAAF career come to a sudden end as its designated successor, the P-51 Mustang, began to arrive in large numbers. By early 1946 no fewer than 339 Spitfires were in long term storage in Australia, waiting for the scrappers to move in. Fifteen of them suffered an arguably worse fate when they were transferred to the Royal Australian Navy in 1948 for use as non-flying ground based trainers. After being butchered and mangled for three to four years, they ended their days being 'burnt to death' on a fire dump.

This well-worn Spitfire LF VIII of No 79 Sqn, RAAF, was photographed between fighter-bomber missions at Biak, New Guinea, in April 1945. Serialled A58-505, it was delivered to the RAAF in July 1944, and proceeded to serve with several frontline and training squadrons until it was 'authorised for writing off', along with most other surviving Mk VIIIs, in May 1946. It was finally struck off charge and scrapped in November 1948

PILOT PROFILES

The following is a brief summary of the seven Australian aces who achieved some or all of their victories whilst flying the Spitfire marks covered in this volume. While some 70 Australian pilots became aces during World War 2, it is noteworthy that none of them added to their scores while flying later model Spitfires in the Pacific. As discussed above, by the time the RAAF had put the Spitfire Mk VIII into general service, meaningful opportunities for kills were becoming very limited due to the operational policies of the time – they primarily flew strafing missions well away from the main Japanese air forces.

Most Australian aces achieved their kills either in the North Africa/Mediterranean campaigns, in Europe or during the early years of the Pacific war flying either Kittyhawks or earlier model Spitfires.

SQN LDR HUGO ARMSTRONG

Hugo Armstrong (nicknamed 'Sinker') was credited with 12 kills during World War 2, all of them on Spitfires and all with RAF squadrons. Of those, the last three were while flying Spitfire Mk IXs with No 611 Sqn at Biggin Hill. Armstong was commissioned as a Pilot Officer in early 1941 and was sent to Britain a short time afterwards. He served with Nos 129 and 72 Sqns until July 1942, when he was posted as OC to No 611 Sqn. In the meantime his tally had reached nine, the first kill occurring on 21 September 1941 when he downed a Bf 109E over Le Touquet while escorting Blenheims in a No 129 Sqn Mk VB.

The move to No 611 Sqn gave Armstrong his first opportunity to fly the Spitfire Mk IX, and all three of his victories on this mark (plus two probables) were scored in the same aircraft, BS435/FY-F. The first of these was recorded on 2 November 1942 when an Fw 190 was claimed destroyed and a Bf 109F was noted as a probable. He claimed another Fw 190 probable on 9 November over Calais on a fighter

A truly evocative shot of Spitfire LF VIII A58-489 escorting a P-38 Lightning of the USAAF off the coast of Morotai in early 1945. This aircraft Also wears the familiar UP codes of No 79 Sqn, as well exhibiting the generally weather-beaten appearance that was synonymous with the overworked Spitfires in this theatre of operations. The temperatures were always hot in the Pacific, and the poky cockpit endured by Spitfire pilots the world over quickly became oppressively hot even when 'on the wing'. This pilot has had to resort to 'opening a window' to improve the ventilation in his fighter, although no doubt this was quickly slammed shut should the chance of combat appear in the offing. The serial A58-489 can just be made out to the left of the letter U, this aircraft having been issued to the RAAF along with 52 other LF VIIIs in July 1944. Sadly, it did not survive the war, crashing into Galela Lake, west of Morotai, in early September 1945 *(via Howard Levy)*

sweep. Two more scores followed on 20 January 1943 – a pair of Bf 109Fs south of Pevensey Bay. These aircraft had been part of a raid on Biggin Hill which remarkably coincided with the base wing (which included No 611 Sqn) coming under the control of Wg Cdr 'Sailor' Malan. In the battle which followed, the squadron managed to shoot down six aircraft, for which Armstrong was credited with two victories.

These were Armstrong's last victories as two weeks later he was shot down and killed over the Channel by a formation of eight Fw 190s of 5./JG 26 while attempting to join a sweep being staged by No 340 Sqn – Ofz Heinz Gomann (13 kills) was credited with the victory.

Wt Off Bobby Bunting

Warrant Officer Bob Bunting became an exclusively Spitfire ace in 1944, notching up five kills with No 93 Sqn during the early months of that year whilst flying Spitfire Mk IXs over Italy. Bunting's first two victories were scored against Fw 190s on 29 February 1944 flying Mk IX MH934/HN-C, following the earlier damaging of another Fw 190 near Anzio nine days previously in the same aircraft. Another 'double' was recorded on 24 March when a pair of Bf 109Gs fell to MH934's guns, followed by a probable against an Fw 190 whilst flying MA687 over Cassino three days later. His final kill occurred four months later when he claimed an Fw 190 whilst flying MA583/HN-C.

Bunting was awarded a British DFC on becoming an ace, and also received an American DFC in recognition of his work covering the landings at Salerno in September 1943.

Flg Off 'Larry' Cronin

Lawrence 'Larry' Cronin was one of the many Australian pilots to graduate from the Empire Air Training Scheme in Australia and then

An anonymous pilot climbs out of Spitfire LF VIII A58-518 at the end of another uneventful sortie from Livingstone, south of Darwin, in mid-1944. From this angle the tropicalised carburettor filter intake is clearly visible underneath the nose, as is the small 30 gallon fuel tank bolted beneath the fuselage – although the latter item was technically an optional fit, it tended to remain attached to the No 1 Wg's fleet of LF VIIIs on a permanent basis. This particular aircraft was eventually lost without trace during a fighter sweep over north-east Borneo in July 1945

Exhibiting subtle differences in both national markings and camouflage details over the other RAAF Spitfire LF VIIIs depicted in this chapter, this five-ship formation was photographed somewhere over New South Wales in mid-1945. Note that the fuselage roundels have far larger centre discs and that the white wing leading edges have been camouflaged over. Although all five aircraft were relatively early-build LF VIIIs, they all survived the war, only to be scrapped soon afterwards

be sent to the UK. His first posting was to No 453 Sqn in August 1942, but he remained with the Australian unit for only two months before transferring to No 81 Sqn. It was here that Cronin scored his five kills, all of them on Spitfires. He moved to North Africa in October 1942 with No 81 Sqn, where the unit initially flew Mk VCs – he damaged a Ju 88 near Bone whilst flying Mk VC 'G' on 3 January 1943. Later that month the first Mk IXs arrived, and after claiming two Bf 109Gs damaged in March and April, Cronin was finally credited with two kills following a mission on 25 July 1943. Flying EN490, he shot down a pair of Bf 109Gs over northern Sicily, and followed up this success on 14 September with an Fw 190 over Salerno, this time while at the controls of Spitfire Mk IX MB807.

No 81 Sqn was then transferred to Burma to fight the Japanese and was re-equipped with Spifire Mk VIIIs upon their arrival at Alipore. Cronin scored his fourth and fifth kills in March 1944 flying JF630/FL-C – a Mitsubishi Ki 46 'Dinah', followed a week later by a Nakajima Ki 43 'Oscar', the latter after a dogfight which had seen him and his wingman bounced by eight Oscars shortly after take-off during a squadron scramble from the forward detachment strip known as 'Broadway'. His wingman was shot down, but Cronin managed to gain height before claiming his fifth and last victim – he also damaged another Ki 43 in the melée. His final score was on 12 April when he claimed an 'Oscar' damaged over Tulihal.

Larry Cronin returned to Australia in late 1944 to teach fighter affiliation tactics at the RAAF's No 1 Operational Training Unit.

SQN LDR RUSSELL FOSKETT

Russell Foskett's career as a pilot ended with 6.5 victories to his credit, all but the last of them scored while flying Hurricanes with No 80 Sqn RAF in the Middle East in 1941/42. He transferred to No 94 Sqn as Commanding Officer in October 1943, who were again based in the Mediterranean and equipped with Hurricane Mk IICs. The squadron re-equipped with Spitfire Mk IXs in February 1944 and it was in MA766/GO-F that Foskett scored his final victory. This occurred on 6 June 1944 when he forced down a Ju 52/3m at Tmimi, in Libya, following a sweep over nearby Crete.

No 94 Sqn swapped its Mk IXs for earlier Mk VB/Cs shortly afterwards and was posted to Greece. It was during a sweep over the Aegean Islands that Foskett was killed when his parachute failed to open following the evacuation of his aircraft after it had suffered engine failure. His body was never found.

SQN LDR TONY GAZE DFC

The flamboyant Tony Gaze ended the war as Australia'a tenth highest scoring fighter ace with 12.5 kills to his credit. All of them were scored when flying Spifires with RAF squadrons operating in Europe. Gaze was in Britain studying at Cambridge when war broke out, prompting him to join the RAF. His first posting was to No 610 Sqn, with whom he scored his first 3.5 kills in 1941 in Spitfire Mk IIs and VBs.

Gaze then transferred as a flight commander to No 616 Sqn who were equipped with the 'rare' high-altitude optimised Spitfire Mk VI. Here he made history on 13 July 1942 when he recorded the variant's first kill, an Fw 190 of 4./JG 26 which was credited to him as a probable. Another Fw 190 and a Do 217 were added to his tally between then and the following month. No further victories were scored by Gaze for another year, before he finally broke the drought with a Fw 190 and a Bf 109G probable in August 1943 whilst flying Spitfire Mk IX MA621 'A' with No 129. A further Fw 190 full kill was scored the following month whilst serving as a flight commander with No 66 Sqn in Mk Vs.

The intervening 12 months had seen Gaze serve a controversially brief tour as CO of No 64 Sqn, equipped with Mk IXs, and then rested, during which time he flew the occassional sortie and worked as a fighter instructor. His posting to No 66 Sqn resulted in the single kill noted above, and his own problems as he was shot down over France. It took him a month to get back to the UK, where he was hostpitalised due to injuries sustained in the shooting down. After recovering, Gaze served with the Air Fighting Development Unit between February and July 1944, but he found this relatively uninteresting and was known to occasionally, and surreptitiously, fly sorties with No 442 Sqn! His repeated requests to return to operational flying finally bore fruit and Gaze was posted to No 610 Sqn in July 1944. This unit was by now equipped with Spitfire Mk XIVs,

and he soon added two more kills to his tally – an Fw 190D on New Year's Day 1945 during Operation *Bödenplatte*, and on 14 February when he downed an Me 262. Gaze's final appointment was with No 41 Sqn in Belgium during the last weeks of the war in Europe. Again flying Mk XIVs, he became a double ace during April by downing a Ju 52/3m (in SM823/EB-E), a shared Ar 234 (RB143), a shared Fw 190D (SM826) and, on 30 April, a solo Fw 190D in SM823. Tony Gaze continued flying after hostilities in Europe had ceased, before he returning to Australia in 1946.

FLT LT WILFRED GOOLD

Wilfred Goold scored five kills during World War 2, all of them with No 607 Sqn in India, and all against Ki 43 'Oscars'. The first was recorded in late 1942 when the unit was equipped with Hurricane IICs, and this was followed in February 1944 with two more in a single action. By this time No 607 were flying Spitfire Mk VCs.

No 607 Sqn re-equipped with Spitfire Mk VIIIs in March 1944, and Goold scored his last two victories in this mark two months later. The first was on 11 May while flying LV755/AF-Z on a patrol over Imphal where he successfully bounced an unsuspecting 'Oscar', and the second occurred a week later during a freewheeling dogfight involving large numbers of aircraft over Palel. Leading the squadron in JG559/AF-N, Goold destroyed one 'Oscar' and damaged two others during the battle. He returned to Australia in June as an instructor.

WG CDR DONALD SMITH

Don Smith joined the RAAF soon after war was declared and first saw action as a Flying Officer attached to No 126 Sqn on Malta after flying in a Spitfire Mk VC off of *Eagle* in mid-1942. He remained on the island until 14 July when he was wounded in action, having scored three kills and two probables in just over a week of combat. Following his recovery, Smith was posted to No 41 Sqn with Spitfire Mk XIIs in 1943, adding one confirmed and one damaged (both Fw 190s) to his score. He took command of No 453 Sqn in April 1944, and led the unit in Spitfire Mk IXBs during the D-Day landings. Smith claimed one Bf 109 confirmed, one probable and two Fw 190s damaged during his time as OC. He returned to Australia in September 1944 with his score standing at five and one shared, two probables and two damaged.

Sqn Ldr Russell Foskett is seen at the controls of early-build Spitfire LF IX MH559 of No 94 Sqn in mid-1944 during a bomber escort mission over the Mediterranean from the unit's Cyrenaica strip at LG147/Bu Amud – a rudimentary site just east of Tobruk. It was in a sister-ship to this aircraft, coded GO-F (serial MA766), that he scored his sixth, and final, kill of the war – a Ju 52m3 on 6 June 1944. Many of the squadron's Spitfires Mk IXs were from an order for Mk VCs placed with Vickers-Armstrongs in May 1942 that were re-engined by Rolls-Royce with the uprated Merlin 61/63 engine and given the new appellation 'Mk IX' *(via Neil Mackenzie)*

APPENDICES

COMPARATIVE TRIAL: SPITFIRE Mk IX v Fw 190A

In July 1942 an early production Spitfire Mk IX fitted with the Merlin 61 engine was flown in a comparative trial against a Focke-Wulf Fw 190 which had been captured intact. Considering the fact that these were two quite different aircraft built to differing operational concepts, the close similarities in performance are remarkable. Excerpts from the trials report are given below.

Comparative Speeds – The Fw 190 was compared with a fully operational Spitfire Mk IX for speed and manoeuvrability at heights up to 25,000 ft. The Spitfire Mk IX at most heights is slightly superior in speed to the Fw 190 and the approximate differences in speeds at various heights are as follows:

At 2000 ft the Fw 190 is 7-8 mph faster than the Spitfire Mk IX

At 5000 ft the Fw 190 and the Spitfire Mk IX are approximately the same

At 8000 ft the Spitfire Mk IX is 8 mph faster than the Fw 190

At 15,000 ft the Spitfire Mk IX is 5 mph faster than the Fw 190

At 18,000 ft the Fw 190 is 3 mph faster than the Spitfire Mk IX

At 21,000 ft the Fw 190 and the Spitfire Mk IX are approximately the same

At 25,000 ft the Spitfire Mk IX is 5-7 mph faster than the Fw 190

Climb – During comparative climbs at various heights up to 23,000 ft, with both aircraft flying under maximum continuous climbing conditions, little difference was found between the two aircraft, although on the whole the Spitfire Mk IX was slightly better.

Above 22,000 ft the climb of the Fw 190 is falling off rapidly, whereas the climb of the Spitfire Mk IX is increasing.

When both aircraft were flying at high cruising speed and were pulled up into a climb from level flight, the Fw 190 had a slight advantage in the initial stages of the climb due to its better acceleration. This superiority was slightly increased when both aircraft were pulled up into the climb from a dive.

It must be appreciated that the differences between the two aircraft are only slight, and that in actual combat the advantage in climb will be with the aircraft that has the initiative.

Dive – The Fw 190 is faster than the Spitfire Mk IX in a dive, particularly during the initial stage. This superiority is not as marked as when the same evasive manoeuvre is flown against the Spitfire Mk VB, however.

Manoeuvrability – The Fw 190 is more manoeuvrable than the Spitfire Mk IX except in turning circles, when it is out-turned without difficulty.

The superior rate of roll of the Fw 190 enabled it to avoid the Spitfire Mk IX if attacked when in a turn, by flicking over into a diving turn in the opposition direction and, as with the Spitfire Mk VB, the Spitfire Mk IX had great difficulty in following this manoeuvre.

It would have been easier for the Spitfire Mk IX to follow the Fw 190 in a diving turn if its engine had been fitted with a negative-G carburettor, as this type of engine with an ordinary carburettor cuts out very easily (the Spitfire used in the trial was an early Mk IX, and later aircraft had negative-G carburettors).

The Spitfire Mk IX's worst heights for fighting the Fw 190 were between 18,000 and 22,000 ft and below 3000 ft. At these heights the Fw 190 is a little faster.

Both aircraft 'bounced' one another in order to ascertain the best evasive tactics to adopt. The Spitfire Mk IX could not be caught when 'bounced' if it was cruising at high speed and saw the Fw 190 when well out of range.

When the Spitfire Mk IX was cruising at low speed its inferiority in acceleration gave the Fw 190 a reasonable chance of catching it up and the same applied if the position is reversed and the Fw 190 was 'bounced' by the Spitfire Mk IX except that overtaking took a little longer.

The initial acceleration of the Fw 190 is better than the Spitfire Mk IX under all conditions of flight, except in level flight at such altitudes where the Spitfire has a speed advantage and then, provided the Spitfire is cruising at high speed, there is very little to choose between the acceleration of the two aircraft.

The general impression gained by the pilots taking part in the trials is that the Spitfire Mk IX compares favourably with the Fw 190 and that provided the Spitfire has the initiative, it had undoubtedly a very good chance of shooting the Luftwaffe fighter down.

COMPARATIVE TRIAL
SPITFIRE Mk XIV COMPARED WITH
THE SPITFIRE Mk IX, Fw 190A AND Bf 109G

Early in 1944 the Air Fighting Development Unit at Duxford flew a Spitfire Mk XIV in comparative trials against a Spitfire Mk IX and captured examples of the Focke-Wulf Fw 190A and the Messerschmitt Bf 109G. Excerpts from the trials report are given below:

Tactical Comparison with the Spitfire Mk IX – The tactical differences are caused by chiefly by the fact that the Spitfire Mk XIV has an engine of greater capacity and is the heavier aircraft (weighing 8400 lbs against 7480 lbs of the Mk IX).

Range and Endurance – The Mk XIV, without a long-range tank, carries 110 gallons of fuel and 9 gallons of oil. When handled similarly, the Mk XIV uses fuel at about 1¼ times the rate of the Mk IX. Its endurance is therefore slightly less. Owing to its higher speed for corresponding engine settings, its range is about equal. For the same reasons, extra fuel carried in a long-range tank keeps its range about equal to that of the Mk IX, its endurance being slightly less.

Speeds – At all heights the Mk XIV is 30-35 mph faster in level flight. The best performance heights are similar, being just below 15,000 ft and between 25,000 and 32,000 ft.

Climb – The Mk XIV has a slightly better maximum climb than the Mk IX, having the best maximum rate of climb yet seen at this unit. In the zoom climb the Mk XIV gains slightly all the way, especially if full throttle is used in the climb.

Dive – The Mk XIV will pull away from the Mk IX.

Turning Circle – The turning circles of both aircraft are identical. The Mk XIV appears to turn slightly better to port than it does to starboard. The warning of the approaching high speed stall is less pronounced in the case of the Mk XIV.

Rate of Roll Rate of roll for both is much the same.

Search View and Rear View – All-round view from the cockpit is good; the longer nose of the aircraft interferes with the all-round visibility, which remains the same as that of the Mk IX. Rear-view is similar.

Conclusions – All-round performance of the Mk XIV is better than the Mk IX at all heights. In level flight it is 25-35 mph faster and has a greater rate of climb. Its manoeuvrability is as good as a Mk IX. It is easy to fly but should be handled with care when taxying and taking off.

COMBAT TRIAL AGAINST THE Fw 190A

Max Speeds – From 0-5000 ft and 15,000-20,000 ft the Mk XIV is only 20 mph faster; at all other heights it is up to 60 mph faster than the Fw 190A. It is estimated to have about the same maximum speed as the new Fw 190 (DB603) at all heights (this was a reference to the more powerful Fw 190D, which would not become operational until late in the summer of 1944).

Max Climb – The Mk XIV has a considerably greater rate of climb than the Fw 190 A or (esti-mated) the new Fw 190 (DB603) at all heights.

Dive – Fw 190 gains slightly initially, but overall the Mk XIV has a slight advantage.

Turning Circle – Mk XIV can easily turn inside the Fw 190, though in the case of a right-hand turn, this difference is not quite so pronounced.

Rate of Roll – Fw 190 is very much better.

Conclusions – In defence, the Mk XIV should use its remarkable maximum climb and turning circle against the enemy. In the attack it can afford to 'mix it' but should beware of the quick roll and dive. If this manoeuvre is used by an Fw 190 and the Mk XIV follows, the latter will probably not close on the Fw 190 until it has pulled out.

Combat Trial Against The Bf 109G

Max Speed – Mk XIV is 40 mph faster at all heights except 16,000 ft; here it is only ten mph faster.

Max Climb – Same result: at 16,000 ft both aircraft are identical, otherwise the Mk XIV out-climbs the Bf 109G. Zoom climb is practically identical when made without opening the throttle. At full throttle, the Mk XIV draws away from the Bf 109G easily.

Dive – During the initial part of the dive, the Bf 109G pulls away slightly, but when a speed of 380 mph is reached, the Mk XIV gains on the Bf 109G.

Turning Circle – Mk XIV out-turns the Bf 109G.

Rate of Roll – Mk XIV rolls much more quickly.

Conclusion – Mk XIV is superior to the Bf 109G.

1

Mk IXC BR369/EH-T of Wg Cdr Eric Thomas, OC Biggin Hill Wing, August 1942

Thomas had built up his score earlier in the war in Spitfires Mk Is, IIs and Vs with Nos 222 and 133 Sqns. He did not add to his total while flying later versions of the fighter. At the end of the war Thomas' final tally was four aircraft destroyed and one shared destroyed, one and one shared probably destroyed and four and one shared damaged.

2

Mk IX EN398/JE-J of Wg Cdr 'Johnnie' Johnson, OC Kenley Wing, spring 1943

Johnson's biography is given in chapter 4. While flying EN398, he was credited with the destruction of 12 aircraft and shared in the destruction of 5 more, inflicted damage on 6 and shared in causing damage to 1 more. Also, on 20 June 1943, Sqn Ldr Robert McNair, OC of No 421 Sqn, was flying EN398 when he shot down an Fw 190.

3

Mk XIV RM787/CG of Wg Cdr Colin Gray, OC flying, Lympne, October 1944

Gray's biography is also given in chapter 4. By war's end his score stood at 27 aircraft destroyed (7 while flying the Mk IX) and 2 shared destroyed, 6 and 4 shared probably destroyed and 12 damaged, making him the top-scoring Kiwi pilot.

4

F VII MD188/PB of Wg Cdr Peter Brothers, OC Culmhead Wing, June 1944

Wearing a two-letter code as well as the standard RAF high altitude fighter scheme of the period – PR Blue upper surfaces and Deep Sky, Type S undersurfaces – this aircraft was one of the last F VIIs built. First flown on 21 May 1944, it was issued to No 131 Sqn in June, but was quickly seconded to the Culmhead Station Flight, and Peter Brothers. Its pilot had fought in France and during the Battle of Britain, and by war's end was credited with 16 aircraft destroyed, 1 probably destroyed and 3 damaged. His last kill was achieved on 7 August 1944 in MD188 against an Fw 190 over France.

5

LF IX PT396/EJ-C of Wg Cdr 'Jack' Charles RCAF, OC Tangmere Wing, August 1944

The frontline was rapidly moving beyond the range of Tangmere's Spitfires by 1944, and Charles failed to gain any kills while flying PT396. By VE-Day his score stood at 15 aircraft destroyed and 1 shared, 6 and 1 shared probably destroyed and 5 damaged – six kills were achieved with the Mk IX, with one being Biggin Hill's 1000th victory.

6

LF IX MK483/VY of Wg Cdr Adolphe Vybiral, OC of the Czech-manned North Weald Wing, 1944

A fighter pilot with the Czech Air Force before the war, Vybiral fled following German occupation and joined the French Air Force. In the Battle of France he flew Curtiss Hawks, claiming seven aircraft destroyed. He did not add to his score in the RAF.

7

Mk VIII A58-464/CR-C of Grp Capt Clive Caldwell, OC No 80 Wg RAAF, Morotai, summer 1945

By mid-1945 Japanese air activity over the South-West Pacific had all but collapsed, and No 80 Wg was engaged mainly in ground strafing operations. Caldwell achieved no victories while flying the Mk VIII, and at the end of the war his score stood at 27 aircraft destroyed and 3 shared, 6 probably destroyed and 15 damaged – these were achieved while flying Tomahawks and Kittyhawks over North Africa, and Spitfire Mk Vs from Darwin. This aircraft initially received the RAF serial JG557 for its flight trials in the UK, flying for the first time on 24 January 1944. Shipped to Australia aboard the *Narbaba* between February and May, it served with No 80 Wg on Morotai, before finally being struck of charge (SOC) in November 1948.

8

Mk VIII A58-497/RG-V of Wg Cdr Robert Gibbes, Deputy Wing Leader No 80 Wg RAAF, Sattler Field, Northern Territory, summer 1944

Gibbes served as deputy to Caldwell. Like the latter, he achieved no victories while flying the Mk VIII due to a dearth of enemy activity in the area. At the end of the war Gibbes' score stood at 10 aircraft destroyed and 2 shared, 5 probably destroyed and 16 damaged, all achieved while flying Tomahawks and Kittyhawks with No 3 Sqn, RAAF, in North Africa. A58-497 failed to make the trip overseas, having been written off by another pilot in a landing accident at Sattler Field, south of Darwin, in December 1944.

9

LF IX MJ845/HBW of Wg Cdr Harold Bird-Wilson, OC No 122 Wg, Funtington, January 1944

An extremely accomplished aviator who has flown no less than 213 different types of aircraft over the years ranging from a Wallis autogiro through to an F-15, Bird-Wilson achieved most of his score in both the Battle of France and Britain with No 17 Sqn. At the end of the war his tally stood at 3 aircraft destroyed and 6 shared destroyed, 3 damaged and 1 destroyed on the ground. Bird-Wilson's last kill was a Bf 109G downed in August 1944 whilst flying a Mk IX with the Harrowbeer Wing.

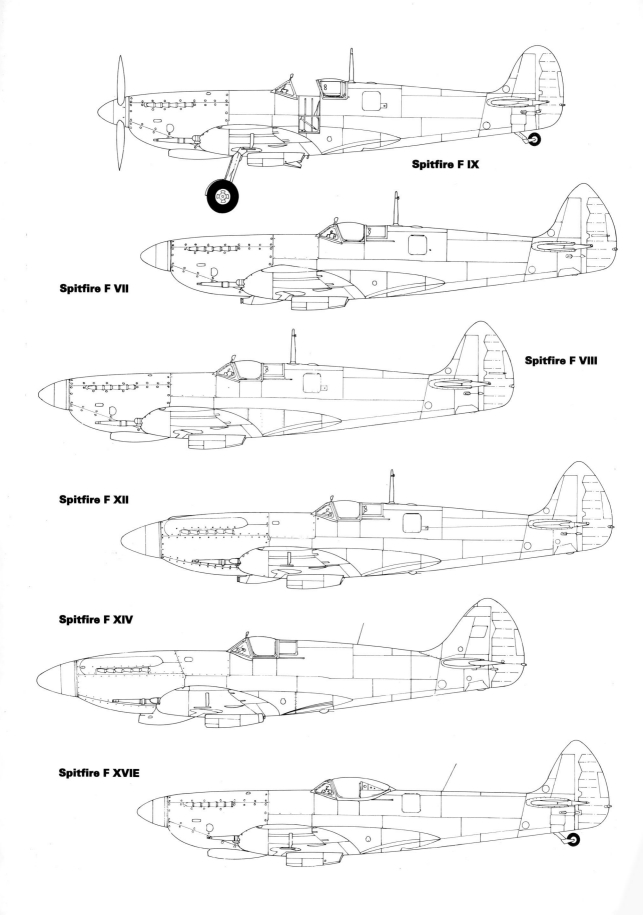

Spitfire F IX

Spitfire F VII

Spitfire F VIII

Spitfire F XII

Spitfire F XIV

Spitfire F XVIE

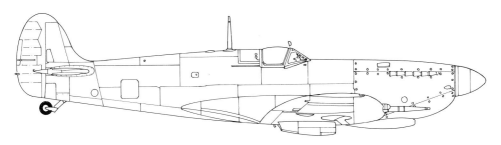

**Spitfire F IXC (early)
(planforms and side-views)**

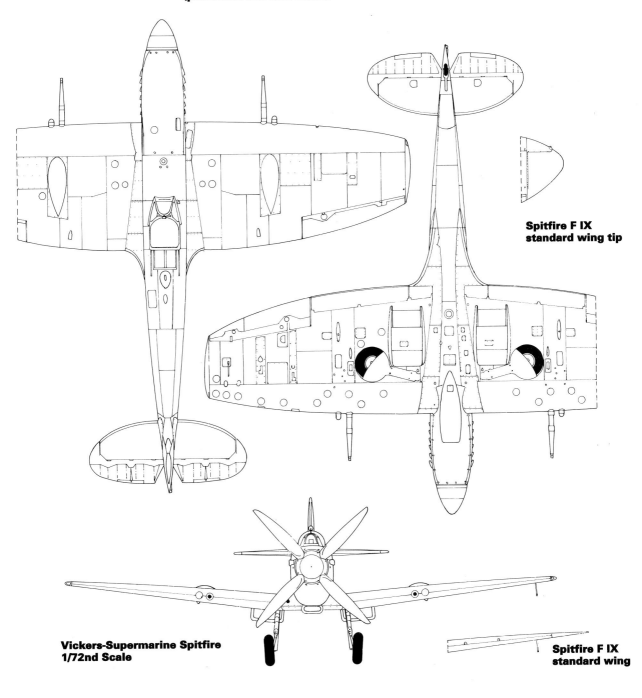

**Spitfire F IX
standard wing tip**

**Vickers-Supermarine Spitfire
1/72nd Scale**

**Spitfire F IX
standard wing**

10

Mk XIVE RM809/GCK of Wg Cdr George Clinton Keefer, OC No 125 Wg, Eindhoven, Holland, March 1945

Keefer was flying this machine when he shot down a Bf 109G near Rheine on 2 March 1945, followed by a Bf 109K of I./JG 27 17 days later. Canadian Keefer had earlier flown Hurricane IIs in the Western Desert with No 274 Sqn, then Spitfires Mk Vs/IXs in England with No 412 Sqn, and finally as leader of No 126 Wg. Given command of the Mk XIV-equipped No 125 Wg in November 1944, Keefer enjoyed success in leading sweeps across Germany in March and April 1945. By war's end his score stood at 12 aircraft destroyed, 2 probably destroyed, 9 damaged and 5 destroyed on the ground. Note how the Fighter Command band on RM809 has been painted out, a move adopted in 1945. From its first flight in September 1944 until it was scrapped in mid-1947, this aircraft served with eight frontline units, most of them Canadian.

11

Mk XIVE MV268/JEJ of Grp Capt 'Johnnie' Johnson, OC No 127 Wg, 2 TAF, Soltau, Germany, May 1945

Johnson took command of the Wing early in April 1945 and by VE-Day, less than a month later, he had encountered few enemy aircraft. As a result he gained no kills in the Mk XIVE. Like RM809, MV268 has had its 'fighter band' painted out.

12

LF IXC MJ783/WX-F of Grp Capt Aleksander Gabszewicz, OC No 131 Wg, 2 TAF, Lille/Vendeville, France, September 1944

First seeing action over Poland in a PZL PXIc on I September 1939, Gabszewicz, claimed a half kill in a He 111 before fleeing to France, where he flew combat sorties in a Bloch MB 152. He eventually ended up in the RAF, and steadily added to his score whilst flying firstly Hurricanes and then Spitfires from 1941 to 43. Gabszewicz's final kills were achieved in Mk IXs as leader of No 2 'Polish' Wg in 1943. He took command of No 131 Wg in July 1944, but failed to add to his score, which at the end of the war stood at eight destroyed and three shared, one and one shared probably destroyed and two damaged. After the war MJ783 was passed onto the Belgian Air Force, and today resides in the Brussels Aviation Museum

13

LF IX ML294/RAB, of Wg Cdr Rolfe Berg, OC No 132 Wg, 2 TAF, Grimbergen, Belgium, December 1944

Norwegian Berg was shot down by flak and killed over Germany on 3 February 1945. His score then stood at six aircraft destroyed and two probably destroyed, three shared damaged and six destroyed on the ground. Most of Berg's total was claimed whilst flying with No 331 Sqn in 1942/43.

14

LF IX MK392 JE-J of Wg Cdr 'Johnnie' Johnson, OC No 144 Wg, Ford, June 1944

This is how Johnson's aircraft looked when he shot down an Fw 190 over France on 16 June 1944. While flying MK392 he was credited with the destruction of 12 aircraft (all Fw 190s and Bf 109s), 1 shared destroyed on the ground (Ju 88) and one damaged. Indeed, the ace's last kill of the war was scored in this aircraft on 27 September 1944. First flown seven months earlier, MK392 saw service with a variety of RCAF units – Nos 441, 443, 403, 416 and 401 Sqns, in that order. It was finally written off during operations from Heesch, in Holland, in March 1945 whilst part of No 401 Sqn.

15

Mk VIII MD371/FB of Grp Capt Robert Boyd, OC No 239 Wg, Baigachi, India, 1944

Although there are rumours that Boyd claimed several aircraft shot down while he was commander of No 239 Wg, the reports appear not to have been preserved officially. His final score stands at 14 aircraft destroyed and 7 shared destroyed, 3 probably destroyed and 7 damaged, all of them achieved flying Spitfire Is/IIs/VAs and Bs between 1940 and 42, prior to being posted to Burma.

16

LF IX MH884/DS of Grp Capt Wilfred Duncan-Smith, OC No 324 Wg, Calvi, Corsica, August 1944

Duncan-Smith was flying MH884 when he led a pair of Spitfires to Ramatuelle, in the south of France, to inspect the first airstrip to come into use there following the Allied invasion. Duncan-Smith's final score stood at 17 aircraft destroyed and 2 shared, 6 and 2 shared probably destroyed and 8 damaged. More than half of his kills were achieved while flying the Mk IX. MH884, was eventually issued to No 72 Sqn in Italy in mid-1945, and it was whilst assigned to this unit that it was in collision with fellow Mk IX NH453, of No 111 Sqn, at Rutterfeld, in Austria, in April 1946 and written off.

17

Mk XIV RN135/YB-A of Sqn Ldr 'Ginger' Lacey, OC No 17 Sqn, Seletar, Singapore, autumn 1945

In other accounts this aircraft has been depicted in profile wearing different camouflage colours, but new photographic evidence has enabled our artist to show these correctly. Lacey's final score was 28 aircraft destroyed, 5 probably destroyed and 9 damaged. His only kill in a late-mark Spitfire was a Ki 43 'Oscar', downed over Burma with a Mk VIII.

18

Mk XII EN237/EB-V of Sqn Ldr Thomas Neil, OC

No 41 Sqn, Hawkinge, spring 1943

Battle of Britain veteran Neil scored all his kills in 1940/41 flying Hurricanes. At the end of the war his tally was 12 aircraft destroyed and 4 shared destroyed, 2 probably destroyed and 1 damaged. This Mk XII was one of the first delivered to No 41 Sqn, arriving in March 1943. It was lost on operations a year later, have accrued a total of just 281.15 flying hours.

19

Mk XII MB882/EB-B of Flt Lt Donald Smith of No 41 Sqn, Friston, April 1944

Smith's details are related in chapter 7. MB882 was the last Mk XII built, and after No 41 Sqn transitioned to Mk XIVs in September 1944, it ended its days at the Flight Leaders School at Milfield.

20

Mk XIVE MV266/EB-J of Sqn Ldr John Shepherd, OC No 41 Sqn, Twente, Holland, April 1945

Shepherd was flying MV266 when he downed his last four kills in spring 1945. His final score was eight aircraft destroyed and five shared destroyed, one and one shared probably destroyed, two and one shared damaged and seven V1s destroyed.

21

Mk IXC BR600/V-SH of Plt Off Donald Kingaby of No 64 Sqn, Hornchurch, July 1942

Kingaby was flying BR600 on 30 July 1942 when he downed the first kill to fall to a Mk IX, as detailed in chapter 1. Built on the same production run as BR581 (see below), BR600 survived many a scrape during the remaining war years only to be sold for scrap, along with EN398/JE-J and dozens of other combat veterans, in November 1949.

22

Mk IXC BR581/Z-SH of Sqn Ldr Wilfred Duncan-Smith, OC of No 64 Sqn, Hornchurch, August 1942

One of the first Mk IXs issued to the RAF, BR581 was lost during the Dieppe operations on 19 August 1942 when shot down by return fire from a Do 217 – Duncan-Smith had already mortally wounded the bomber by this stage. Its pilot baled out and he was rescued from the sea by naval patrol boat. Duncan-Smith shot down three and claiming a further two shared kills in BR581.

23

F VIII JF502/QJ-F of Flt Lt 'Eddie' Edwards of No 92 Sqn, Marcianise, Italy, early 1944

Canadian Edwards total stood at 15 aircraft destroyed and 3 shared destroyed, 8 and 1 shared probably destroyed and 13 damaged, 9 destroyed on the ground and 5 damaged on the ground. Most of his kills were scored in 1942/43 while flying Kittyhawks over North Africa, although he did claim three and two shared in Mk VIIIs.

24

Mk IX MH934/HN-C of Wt Off Bobby Bunting of No 93 Sqn, Lago, Italy, in February 1944

Bunting's autobiography is given in chapter 7. His mount wore his personal insignia beneath the cockpit, and it was in this machine that he shot down four aircraft and damaged a fifth.

25

Mk IX MA766/GO-F of Sqn Ldr Russell Foskett, OC No 94 Sqn, LG147/Bu Amud, Cyrenaica, June 1944

Foskett's full history is also given in chapter 7. He used MA766 to claim his final kill – a Ju 52m3 on D-Day – and it was written off by another pilot barely a month later.

26

Mk IX MA481/JU-O of Flg Off Irving 'Hap' Kennedy of No 111 Sqn, Falcone, Sicily, September 1943

Canadian Kennedy was flying this machine on the 10 September kill described in chapter 4. His eventual score was 10 aircraft destroyed, 5 shared destroyed and 1 probably destroyed. At the time of the action this Spitfire was brand new, having been delivered only a few days earlier. It went on to enjoy a remarkably long combat career of nearly 20 months before it was lost on operations in April 1945.

27

F VII MD139/ON-W of Flg Off Walter Hibbert of No 124 Sqn, Bradwell Bay, June 1944

MD139 was used by Hibbert when he shared in the destruction of a Bf 109 over France on 12 June 1944. His final score stood at four aircraft destroyed and two shared destroyed, two damaged in the air and two more on the ground.

28

LF IX ML214/5J-K of Sqn Ldr John Plagis, OC No 126 Sqn, Culmhead, July 1944

Plagis was flying this aircraft when he shot down a Bf 109G over France on 24 July 1944 – two other kills and a half share also fell to its guns whilst flown by Plagis. Earlier, he flew Spitfire Mk Vs over Malta with Nos 249 and 185 Sqns, then with No 64 Sqn in the UK. At the end of the war his score stood at 15 aircraft destroyed and 2 shared destroyed, 2 shared probably destroyed, 6 damaged and 1 shared damaged.

29

Mk IX MA621/DV-A of Flt Lt F 'Tony' Gaze of No 129 Sqn, Hornchurch, August 1943

Gaze was flying this aircraft on 17 August 1943 when he shot down an Fw 190 near Antwerp. His full biography is given in chapter 7. MA621 was later issued to No 332 Sqn, before finding its way to an Air Service Training unit in March 1944, where it was written off in a crash in July 1945.

30
F VII MD120/NX-O of Sqn Ldr James O'Meara, OC No 131 Sqn, Colerne, March 1944
Battle of Britain pilot O'Meara flew with Nos 64, 72, and 91 Sqns, before assuming command of No 131 Sqn in March 1943 – he failed to score with this unit, however.His tally stood at 11 aircraft destroyed and 2 shared destroyed, 4 probably destroyed, 11 and 1 shared damaged.

31
Mk XIVE RN133/FF-B of Sqn Ldr Kenneth Charney, OC No 132 Sqn, Madura, India, August 1945
Charney's kills came either during his tour on Mk Vs on Malta with No 185 Sqn in 1942, or two years later on Mk IXs in the UK with Nos 602 and 132 Sqns. His final score was six aircraft destroyed, four probably destroyed and seven damaged.

32
Mk IX EN459/ZX-1 of Flt Lt Eugeniusz Horbaczewski of the Polish Fighting Team, attached to No 145 Sqn, Tunisia, spring 1943
Horbaczewski was shot down and killed by Fw 190s on 18 August 1944 in a Mustang III, his score standing at 16 aircraft destroyed and 1 shared destroyed, 1 probably destroyed and 1 damaged. Most were scored in Mk VBs and IXs in 1942/43.

33
Mk IX EN315/ZX-6 of Sqn Ldr Stanislaw Skalski, OC of the Polish Fighting Team attached to No 145 Sqn, Tunisia, spring 1943
Skalski opened his score over Poland in 1939 when he was credited with six kills. During the Battle of Britain he flew Hurricanes with No 501 Sqn, then went on to fly Spitfires with Nos 306 and 316 Sqns. He was given command of a Mustang III Wing in mid-1944. By May 1945 his score stood at 21 (some say 24) aircraft destroyed, 1 probably destroyed, and 5 damaged. Skalski claimed three kills and one damaged with the PFT.

34
Mk IXC BS451/RF-M of Sqn Ldr Jan Falkowski, OC No 303 Sqn, Northolt, June 1943
Falkowski first flew Hurricanes with No 32 Sqn, then went to Spitfire Mk IIs and Vs with No 315 Sqn. By VE-Day he had scored nine aircraft destroyed and one probably destroyed – two and one probable were scored whilst flying Mk IXs.

35
HF IX ML296/DU-N of Flt Lt Otto Smik of No 312 Sqn, Lympne, September 1944
Smik flew with Nos 122 and 222 Sqns in 1943, scoring a number of victories during this time. In November 1944 he was downed by flak and killed, his score then standing at eight aircraft destroyed, two shared destroyed, two probably destroyed, and three damaged, plus three V1s destroyed.

36
Mk IX BS167/FN-D of Flt Lt Ragnar Dogger of No 331 Sqn, North Weald, July 1943
Dogger was flying BS167 when he damaged a Bf 109 over France on 1 July 1943. A Norwegian, he spent the whole of his operational career with this unit flying Mk IXs and IXBs. By May 1945 Dogger's score stood at six aircraft destroyed and one damaged. BS167 later served with No 229 Sqn, and it was lost whilst flying with this unit on 11 June 1944 on a sweep over Normandy.

37
Mk IXC BS248/AH-O of Sgt Ola Aanjesen of No 332 Sqn, North Weald, summer 1943
Commissioned later in 1943, Aanjesen rose to command No 332 Sqn in April 1945. At the end of the war his score stood at five aircraft destroyed and one shared destroyed, one damaged, one V1 destroyed and one shared destroyed on the ground – all on Mk IXs. The unit badge appears under the cockpit of this aircraft.

38
Mk IX BS393/GW-Z of Lt Michel Boudier of No 340 Sqn, Biggin Hill, October 1942
Boudier was flying this aircraft when he damaged an Fw 190 over the English Channel on 27 October 1942 – he downed another Fw 190 in BS393 two months later. Later in the war this Frenchman flew with No 341 Sqn, with whom he was shot down and wounded on D-Day over Normandy. Despite determined efforts to avoid capture he was made a PoW three weeks later. At that time his score stood at eight aircraft destroyed and seven damaged.

39
Mk IX BS538/NL-B of Sgt Pierre Clostermann of No 341 Sqn, Biggin Hill, June 1943
The Frenchman was flying this converted Mk V when he damaged a Bf 109 over France on 17 June 1943, thus opening his tally. His claim of 33 kills is refuted by historians who have studied official records. Some scores in which he claimed shares were downed by others in his unit when Clostermann, though in the area, did not fire his guns. According to the most reliable figures his score was 11 shot down (plus possibly 7 more), with 2 (plus possibly 3 more) probably destroyed, 9 damaged and 2 destroyed on the ground.

40
Mk XIVE SM825/MN-M of Sqn Ldr Harold Walmsley, OC No 350 Sqn, Celle, Germany, April 1945
On both 24 and 25 April 1945 Walmsley shot down Fw 190s in SM825 over Germany. By war's end his tally stood at 11 aircraft destroyed and 1 shared

destroyed, 1 probably destroyed, 4 damaged and 2 destroyed on the ground.

41

FR XIVE RM785/T of Sqn Ldr William Klersy, OC No 401 Sqn, Wunstorf, Germany, May 1945

RM785 was a fighter-recce version with the oblique camera mounted to look sideways from the starboard side of the fuselage. One of the top scorers in the RCAF, and also in the 2 TAF during the period from D-Day to the end of the war, Klersy was killed in a flying accident in RM785 shortly after VE-Day. His score then stood at 14 aircraft destroyed in the air, 2 destroyed on the ground, 1 shared destroyed and 3 damaged, all on Mk IXs.

42

LF IX ML420/KH-D of Flt Lt James Lindsay of No 403 Sqn, Tangmere, June 1944

On 26 June 1944 Lindsay damaged a Bf 109 over Normandy in ML420. A Canadian, he flew F-86s in Korea in 1952 and was credited with two MiG-15s kills and two damaged. His score was eight aircraft destroyed (six in WW 2) and one shared destroyed, and eight damaged (six in WW 2).

43

LF IXE RR201/DB-A of Flt Lt Dick Audet of No 411 Sqn, Heesch, Holland, December 1944

This was the LF IXE flown by Audet during the remarkable sortie on 29 December 1945, detailed in chapter 6. By January 31 he had doubled his score, but was killed on 3 March 1945 when he was downed by flak after strafing a railway siding. His final score was 10 aircraft destroyed and 1 shared destroyed, 1 aircraft damaged and 1 destroyed on the ground.

44

Mk VIII JF469/AN-M of Flt Lt Albert Houle of No 417 Sqn, Gioia del Colle, Italy, October 1943

Houle was flying JF469 on 4 October 1943 when he shot down an Fw 190 of III./SKG 10, and damaged two others, east of Rome. Canadian Houle had flown Hurricanes IICs over the Western Desert with No 213 Sqn. By war's end his score was 11 aircraft destroyed and 1 shared destroyed, 1 probably destroyed and 7 damaged.

45

Mk IX BS152/AU-P of Sqn Ldr Robert McNair OC No 421 Sqn, Kenley, June 1943

McNair downed an Fw 190 over France on 24 June 1943 in BS152. A Canadian, by war's end his score was 16 aircraft destroyed, 5 probably destroyed and 14 damaged.

46

LF IX MK399/9G-K of Flt Lt Frederick Wilson of No 441 Sqn, Westhampnett, May 1944

Wilson was flying MK339 when he downed an Fw 190 over France on 5 May 1944. Also a Canadian, he flew Hurricanes with No 80 Sqn over Syria and with No 213 Sqn over the Western Desert. At the end of the war his score stood at eight aircraft destroyed and one shared destroyed, two probably destroyed, five damaged in the air, and four destroyed on the ground.

47

Mk IX MK321/2I-H of Sqn Ldr Henry McLeod, OC No 443 Sqn, Westhampnett, April 1944

Yet another RCAF ace, McLeod's biography is given in chapter 4. He shot down a Do 217 in MK321 on 19 April 1944 – six days later it too was lost when it ran out of fuel and belly landed at Puddleton, Dorset.

48

Mk IX EN522/FU-F of Sqn Ldr John Ratten, OC No 453 Sqn, Hornchurch, April 1943

On 8 April 1943 Ratten damaged an Fw 190 over France in EN522. An Australian, he continued to fly this aircraft with the same markings, but with a Wing Commander's pennant on the fuselage, following promotion to that rank in May, and his appointment as leader of the Hornchurch Wing. Killed in action in February 1945, his final score stood at two aircraft destroyed and two shared destroyed, one shared probably destroyed, and two damaged. EN522 started life as a Mk V and was converted to Mk IX standard by Rolls-Royce, hence the non-standard nose camouflage.

49

LF IX MJ239/LO-B of Flt Lt Kenneth Charney of No 602 Sqn, Longues, Normandy, July 1944

Charney shot down an Fw 190 near Lisieux on 14 July 1944 in this Spitfire.

50

Mk VIII JG559/AF-N of Flt Lt Wilfred Goold of No 607 Sqn, Imphal, May 1944

This is the aircraft in which Goold shot down a Ki 43 'Oscar' and damaged two others over Palel on 18 May 1944. His details are given in chapter 7.

51

Mk XIV RB159/DW-D of Sqn Ldr R Newbery, OC No 610 Sqn, West Malling, 1944

While commanding the unit in the 'Diver' summer of 1944, Newbery was credited with the destruction of seven V1s over Kent in this Mk XIV.

52

Mk IX BS435/FY-F of Sqn Ldr Hugo Armstrong, OC No 611 Sqn, Biggin Hill, February 1942

Australian Armstrong's favourite Mk IX, he enjoyed success in BS435 (three confirmed and two probables) prior to being killed in it on 5

February 1943 after being bounced over the Channel by eight Fw 190s of II./JG 26. Armstrong's biography is given in chapter 7.

53
LF IX EN572/FY-H of Flt Lt John Checketts of No 611 Sqn, Biggin Hill, May 1943
Checketts gained most of his score in EN572, a Rolls-Royce-converted Mk V. A New Zealander, Checketts was shot down in this aircraft over France on 6 September 1943, but was smuggled back to England seven weeks later – he returned to the frontline in mid-1944. Varying sources give different figures for his score at war's end: between 13 and 15 aircraft destroyed, 2 or 3 probably destroyed and 8 damaged, plus 2 V1s destroyed.

54
Mk IX MA419/N-V of Flt Lt Warren Schrader of No 1435 Sqn, Brindisi, Italy, December 1943
Schrader was flying MA419 on 17 December 1943 when he downed two Bf 109Gs off the Albanian coast. Formed from No 1435 Flt at Luqa, Malta, the unit's number was allocated unofficially, as was its identification letter V. By the end of the war Kiwi Schrader had claimed 11 aircraft destroyed and 2 shared destroyed, and 4 destroyed on the ground.

55
Mk IX BF273 of Flg Off Emanuel Galitzine of the High Altitude Flight, Northolt, September 1942
Galitzine's combat in BF273 is described in chapter 1. The Mk IX had been specially modified for operations at altitude, and had the machine guns, armour and other unnecessary items removed. It was painted in a non-standard scheme.

56
Mk VIII CM-M of Lt Col Charles 'Sandy' McCorkle, OC 31st FG, US 12th Air Force, Castel Volturno, Italy, January 1944
McCorkle's score stood at three aircraft destroyed at this point. Later, the 31st FG rec-eived with Mustangs, and by the end of the war his tally was 11 victories, 5 while flying Spitfires.

57
Mk VIII HL-X of Lt Leland Molland, 308th FS, 31st FG, US 12 Air Force, Castel Volturno, Italy, January 1944
The white swastika under the cockpit denoted his confirmed victory at that time and the five black ones probable kills. By war's end his score was 11½ victories, 4 of them while flying Spitfires.

58
F VIII JF626/AX-W of Maj Henry Gaynor, No 1 Sqn SAAF, Italy, December 1943
Gaynor, a South African, claimed the last of his five kills in this aircraft on 2 December 1943 when he downed an Fw 190. A veteran of North Africa, he flew with the same unit from 1942 until his death in a flying accident in March 1944 – he hit a high tension cable during a low-level sweep of Italy. Gaynor was OC at No 1 Sqn at the time.

FIGURE PLATES

1
Wg Cdr Peter Brothers, OC Culmhead Wing 1944, wears typical attire for the 1944/45 period. He is dressed in standard issue blue-grey Battledress, over which sits an untied Life Jacket Mk I. Brothers' boots are 1941 Pattern issue, whilst his helmet is a Type C, equipped with Mk VII goggles. The polkadot silk scarf was presented to him by his wife in 1939, and he still has it today!

2
Sqn Ldr 'Jack' Charles, OC No 611 Sqn, as he appeared in May 1943. Wearing similar attire to Peter Brothers, only his earlier Mk IV goggles are different. Notice how the life jacket was tied.

3
New Yorker Flt Lt Henry Zary (five kills), flight commander with No 421 Sqn in July 1944. He is wearing a regulation bright pale blue shirt and black tie, the former being rolled up while out of the cockpit due to the warm summer heat. His footwear also reflects the season – toe-capped black shoes as opposed to heavy flying boots.

4
Capt Ragnar Dogger of No 331 Sqn in June 1944. He wears Royal Norwegian Air Force insignia on his service issue cap and pilot's brevet, a 'Norway' title on his left sleeve and flag badge on his right, captain's stars on his battle dress and a DFC ribbon above the left breast pocket. Dogger's boots are 1943 Pattern.

5
Wg Cdr 'Johnnie' Johnson, OC No 144 Wg, in the summer of 1944. Wearing a standard service issue cap and early pattern RAF battledress blouse adorned with ribbons for the DSO and two bars, DFC and bar 1939-43 Star and US DFC, Johnson's 'civvy' flannels and shoes are most definitely non-regulation! His 'Mae West' is of late issue, whilst his helmet is a Type C.

6
Kiwi Sqn Ldr Colin Gray, OC No 81 Sqn in North Africa in 1943. Over his khaki drill shorts and shirt he is wearing a late pattern life jacket, seat-type parachute and K-Type dinghy pack and RAF webbing belt, with a pistol case and pouch for a .38 revolver. His helmet is a Type D tropical issue, equipped with Mk VII goggles. Like Zary, his footwear augers on the side of comfort.